Brazil

A Culinary Journey

The Hippocrene Cookbook Library

Afghan Food & Cookery
African Cooking, Best of Regional
Albanian Cooking, Best of
Alps, Cuisines of The
Aprovecho: A Mexican-American Border
  Cookbook
Argentina Cooks!, Exp. Ed.
Austrian Cuisine, Best of, Exp. Ed.
Bolivian Kitchen, My Mother's
Burma, Flavors of
Cajun Women, Cooking with
Calabria, Cucina di
Caucasus Mountains, Cuisines of the
Chile, Tasting
Colombian Cooking, Secrets of
Croatian Cooking, Best of, Exp. Ed.
Czech Cooking, Best of, Exp. Ed.
Danube, All Along The, Exp. Ed.
Dutch Cooking, Art of, Exp. Ed.
Egyptian Cooking
Filipino Food, Fine
Finnish Cooking, Best of
French Caribbean Cuisine
French Fashion, Cooking in the (Bilingual)
Germany, Spoonfuls of
Greek Cuisine, The Best of, Exp. Ed.
Gypsy Feast
Haiti, Taste of, Exp. Ed.
Havana Cookbook, Old (Bilingual)
Hungarian Cookbook
Icelandic Food & Cookery
India, Flavorful (Gujarati)
Indian Spice Kitchen
International Dictionary of Gastronomy
Irish-Style, Feasting Galore
Italian Cuisine, Treasury of (Bilingual)
Japanese Home Cooking
Korean Cuisine, Best of
Laotian Cooking, Simple
Latvia, Taste of
Lithuanian Cooking, Art of

Macau, Taste of
Middle Eastern Kitchen, The
Mongolian Cooking, Imperial
New Hampshire: from Farm to Kitchen
New Jersey Cookbook, Farms and Foods
  of the Garden State:
Norway, Tastes and Tales of
Persian Cooking, Art of
Pied Noir Cookbook: French Sephardic
  Cuisine from Algeria
Poland's Gourmet Cuisine
Polish Cooking, Best of, Exp. Ed.
Polish Country Kitchen Cookbook
Polish Cuisine, Treasury of (Bilingual)
Polish Heritage Cookery, Ill. Ed.
Polish Traditions, Old
Portuguese Encounters, Cuisines of
Pyrenees, Tastes of
Quebec, Taste of
Rhine, All Along The
Romania, Taste of, Exp. Ed.
Russian Cooking, Best of, Exp. Ed.
Scandinavian Cooking, Best of
Scottish-Irish Pub and Hearth Cookbook
Sephardic Israeli Cuisine
Sicilian Feasts
Smorgasbord Cooking, Best of
South African Cookery, Traditional
South American Cookery, Art of
South Indian Cooking, Healthy
Sri Lanka, Exotic Tastes of
Swedish Kitchen, A
Swiss Cookbook, The
Syria, Taste of
Taiwanese Cuisine, Best of
Thai Cuisine, Best of, Regional
Turkish Cuisine, Taste of
Ukrainian Cuisine, Best of, Exp. Ed.
Uzbek Cooking, Art of
Vietnamese Kitchen
Warsaw Cookbook, Old

Brazil
A Culinary Journey

Cherie Hamilton

HIPPOCRENE BOOKS
NEW YORK

Book and jacket design by Acme Klong Design, Inc.

Cover photography by Madeline Polss.
All other photography by Kats Barry.
Illustrations by Russell Malcolm Hamilton.

For more information, address:
HIPPOCRENE BOOKS, INC.
171 Madison Avenue
New York, NY 10016

ISBN 0-7818-1080-9
Cataloging-in-Publication Data available from the Library of Congress.
Printed in the United States of America.

Preface

As I note in the preface to my *Cuisines of Portuguese Encounters* (Hippocrene Books, 2001), in 1960 I journeyed to Brazil for the first time. The intent was to spend one year there with my husband, at the time a graduate student Fullbright fellow, and our three-year-old daughter. We ended up staying for nearly three years. During that delightful extended stay, I became quite well acquainted with Brazilian cuisine. Although we lived in the city of Salvador in the state of Bahia, I was able to travel to other regions of that vast South American country.

So felicitous was my introduction to Brazilian cuisine that when I wasn't teaching math at the Pan American School and English as a second language, I was learning how to prepare dishes and researching the history of Brazil's culinary traditions.  Jorge Amado, one of Brazil's most eminent novelists was so taken with my culinary interests that he aided me in my efforts and encouraged me to write a cookbook profiling the cuisine of his native Bahia.

What finally resulted some four decades later was the publication of *Cuisines of Portuguese Encounters*, which encompasses the Portuguese-speaking world, including Brazil. *Sabores da lusofonia. Encontros de Culturas: Angola; Brasil; Cabo Verde; Goa; Guiné-Bissau; Macau; Moçambique; Portugal, Açores e Madeira; São Tomé e Príncipe; Timor Leste*, (Flavors of the Lusophone World. Cultural Encounters: Angola; Brazil; Cape Verde; Goa; Guinea-Bissau; Macao; Mozambique; Portugal; Açores and Madeira; São Tomé and Príncipe; and East Timor) published in April 2005, is a Portuguese language version of this book. *Brazil: A Culinary Journey* which encompasses the country's five regions, does in a way follow Jorge Amado's recommendation in that the late, great writer planted the seed that resulted in this cookbook.

Later I spent a year in Portugal and then in the former Portuguese colonies in Africa and learned that many of the dishes we know today as Brazilian have continental Portuguese, African, and Asian origins. I also learned that native

Brazilian agricultural products and foodways had left their mark on the dishes and alimentary habits of Portugal and its former African and Asian colonies and territories. Portuguese navigators and adventurers served as intermediaries for the spread of New World as well as European, African, and Asian crops, culinary practices, and recipes throughout their empire as well as to other parts of the world.

I have been fortunate in having had the opportunity to visit Brazil on numerous occasions over the decades. During these visits I have continued my research on the nature and history of Brazilian cuisine.

Over these forty years so many have aided me that it would take several pages just to list them by name. Needless to say, I am extremely grateful to all those who helped make this book possible. In the brief remarks that precede many of the individual recipes brought together in this volume I do refer to those who played especially key roles by introducing me to or teaching me how best to prepare a given dish.

In these prefatory remarks I would be remiss, however, if I did not acknowledge by name those key players as well as others not mentioned in the recipe lead-ins but who also contributed to the completion of this project. I owe a debt of gratitude to the late Waldeloir Rego, an esteemed friend and an expert on Bahian food culture who introduced me to the food of the Afro-Brazilian sects known as Condomblé. A friend who taught me how to prepare many Bahian specialties is Veranúbia Barbosa, owner of Nirá, a wonderful health food restaurant in the city of Salvador. And Alício, owner of Salvador's Maria Mata Mouro Restaurant also taught me how to prepare some local dishes. I would be remiss if I did not mention the late Norma Sampaio, who from 1960 to 1962 helped me to improve my Portuguese and who frequently invited me into her kitchen to learn how to make those dishes for which Bahia is so renowned.

Others in Bahia to whom I also owe a debt of gratitude: Nancy Bernabó, wife of the esteemed painter Carybé and their daughter Sossó; João Reis and Mariangela Nogueira, Sílvio and Lia Robatto, the Yaba Sisters—Angela and Elizabeth Mattos, Jose Carlos Limeira, Deoscóredes Maximilliano dos Santos (a.k.a. Mestre Didi), Maria Sampaio, Celia Aguilar, and Florentina Souza.

I also express heartfelt appreciation to my friends in Rio: Laura Padilha, Carmen Lúcia Tindó Ribeiro Secco, Teresa Salgado and Marco António Guimarães da Silva, Mariza Carvalho, Anthony Naro (a U.S. transplant), and Fernanda Felisberto. I am grateful for the help of friends in São Paulo: Benjamin Abdala, Jr., Rita Chaves and her husband José Luis Cabaço, Tánia Macedo, Fabio Lucas (originally from Minas Gerais), and the Antonio Carelli family (Mrs. Isabel Buitor, Fabiana, and Gabriela). In the city of Belo Horizonte, Minas Gerais, my special thanks to Maria Nazareth Fonseca, Susana Pavão, Maria do Carmo Lanna Figueiredo, Maria José dos Santos, and Marli Fantini.

In the United States I would like to thank António Matinho, director and editor-in-chief, and Maria do Carmo Pereira, associate news editor of *Luso-Americano*, Newark, New Jersey's Portuguese-language newspaper who helped promote my first book.

Finally, much appreciation to my husband Russell, my family, neighbors, and other friends who taste-tested these recipes, and to all those, too numerous to name, who gave me encouragement and support throughout my work on this gratifying project.

Cherie Y. Hamilton
Nashville, TN
April, 2005

Table of Contents

Introduction

This cookbook constitutes a culinary journey through South America's largest and most populous country. What might be termed traditional Brazilian cuisine came about through the contributions of several peoples, most notably the native Indians, African slaves and their descendents, and, of course, the Portuguese colonizers.

Just as in the United States and other geographically large, populous, and multiethnic countries, there are several distinctively regional cuisines in Brazil. Regional diversity notwithstanding, there are also what can be termed typically Brazilian dishes, prepared and enjoyed in homes and restaurants throughout the country. Many of these national dishes do vary from region to region with respect to ingredients and modes of preparation. While some of these foods were, obviously, part of the Amerindian diet long before the arrival of the Europeans and Africans, European colonizers and African slaves introduced foods and culinary customs that in time came to constitute, along with the indigenous crops and foodways, what is today a distinctive, multi-faceted national cuisine.

THE AMERINDIAN CONTRIBUTION

In considering the cuisine of Brazil's indigenous peoples (the Amerindians) one must take into account that by the mid 1900s the Amazon region alone was home to more than six hundred tribal nations. Today the approximately 250,000 Amerindians who live in northern Brazil speak as many as 180 different languages. A multiplicity of tribal groups, languages, cultures, foods, and ways of cooking all make it rather difficult to define a single Amerindian Brazilian cuisine.

The diet of the Indians who lived in the Amazon region consisted mainly of cassava and fish from the surrounding waters. From the cassava, which they grated and pounded to a pulp, they made a type of bread that they baked in clay ovens. The pulp was also dried, toasted, crumbled and eaten with fish that had been smoked and roasted on a wooden rack over a fire. They would also grind the roasted fish and mix it with the roasted cassava to serve as rations for hunters. Wild boars, traveling in herds, were hunted by the tribes in the central region. The meat was similarly roasted and smoked, then pounded and mixed with cassava meal.

Corn, also native to the new world, was another staple of the Amerindian diet. The Tupi Guarani Indians ground the corn to make a porridge and fermented it to make an alcoholic drink. Fruit was seasonally plentiful. Some of the more popular fruits were cashew (from which we get the cashew nut), pineapples, avocados, plantains and a variety of bananas.

Other additions to the Tupi diet included peppers of many varieties, the leaves of the cassava plant, turtles and their eggs, lizards, snakes, termites, and large female ants. Cacao seeds were roasted, ground, and shaped into loaves that were then grated and added to drinking water. It was in this same way that the stimulant guarana, made from the fruit of the same name, was consumed.

This indigenous diet, which may seem somewhat odd to us, was certainly nourishing and savory. It fed a migrant people who inhabited semi-permanent camps before the arrival of the Europeans.

THE PORTUGUESE CONTRIBUTION

The Portuguese, of course, played a central role in the establishment of what can be called traditional Brazilian cuisine. Their contribution is easily documented in spite of the influence over the years of a plethora of other Europeans, including the descendents of immigrants from Italy, Germany, Poland, and Spain. The Portuguese possessed an age-old knowledge of cookery and its practices from products that they carried from trading posts and the areas they colonized. The most important of these were the Azores and the Cape Verde archipelago, the latter having served as an entrepot for foods, customs, economic, and culinary habits.

When the Portuguese first reached the territory that would become known as Brazil, they found that the food eaten by the natives was eaten either raw, lightly cooked, or roasted. Their diet, in Portugal was based on rice, couscous, noodles, fava beans, tripe, fish and shellfish, bread, and cheese, and it took them some time to adapt to the foods of this new land. They initially traded some of the rations brought with them for previously unknown exotic fruits and vegetables. Slowly they assimilated a number of the indigenous foods into their own diet. Manioc, which the Portuguese found similar to the European yam, was one of the first crops to be adopted. They also learned how to smoke and roast fish and game and use cassava meal as an accompaniment to meat. The native peoples were less inclined to adopt the foods brought by the Portuguese mariners, but with time such foods as squash, sweet potatoes, lettuce, and a variety of beans entered into the indigenous diet. By the 1800s, mills were in operation and produced various types of sugar, molasses, and alcoholic beverages for human consumption, as well as byproducts that were used as feed for cattle and other farm animals that the Portuguese introduced in Brazil. And with the establishment of the Catholic church and the construction of convents, the nuns who were famous in Portugal for their egg-based sweets, continued with their tradition as confectioners by making doughnuts, puddings, cakes, and egg-based desserts.

When mining was introduced in the southeast region, food supplies had to be brought in from other areas to feed the miners. Through the importation and sale of foodstuffs such as sausages, ham, olive oil, cheese, marmalades, vinegar, and alcoholic beverages, specifically wine, new eating habits were created and cookery took on a different form. The Portuguese introduced their taste for tomatoes and potatoes to this new diet, two foods that were indispensable to Portuguese cooks as ingredients in soups and cod dishes. Portuguese farmers also introduced the cultivation of crops such as rice in Brazil. Coffee was introduced in the sixteenth century and by the end of the 1800s the production of that African crop had expanded, and there were plantations as far south as Minas Gerais and São Paulo.

Brazilian cookery slowly took on a European flavor during the various stages of the ensuing gastronomic revolution. But the flavor was tempered by the African as well as Amerindian influences.

THE AFRICAN CONTRIBUTION

In the late sixteenth century the Portuguese introduced sugarcane to the northeast region of Brazil which they brought from Southeast Asia. The first sugar plantation was established in the state of Pernambuco and this opened the way for more plantations which drew more settlers to the Northeast region. These settlers brought in African slaves who became a dynamic factor in transforming the culture and establishing that region's cuisine. Eating habits, always open to change, were influenced by the culinary customs that the slaves brought with them. The cuisine that began to take shape was also known as *comida de azeite* (food with oil), referring to the palm oil that is still an important ingredient in a number of dishes found in the Northeast. This palm oil, known as *dendê* or *dendem*, is extracted from the pulp of the fruit of a species of the *dendê* palm tree. This particular type of palm tree that produces a red fruit, was brought to Brazil from Africa in the early seventeenth century and was soon planted throughout the Northeast. The red oil extracted from the fruit of the palm gave a color and flavor to Afro-Brazilian food that helped define Africa's participation in Brazilian cookery. Palm oil was not the only African contribution. Although the hot peppers used in Bahian food are of pre-Colombian American origin, they were taken to Africa in the sixteenth century and returned to the northeastern Brazil with African slaves in the seventeenth century.

By the late seventeenth and early eighteenth centuries many African dishes, already common in Brazil, were sold by slaves on the streets of the city of Salvador, Bahia. Some of the foods sold were *acarajé* (black-eyed pea fritters), *abará* (baked black-eyed pea cakes), *caruru* (shrimp and okra stew), *vatapá* (shrimp and bread pudding)—the recipes for which are included in this volume—sweet corn puddings, rice cakes, corn cakes, sweet rolls, and a number of other desserts. Today, many of these foods are still sold on street corners by women dressed in the traditional white lace blouse and skirt worn by members of the Afro-Brazilian religious sects, *Condomblé*.

During this same period the religious system of the slaves of *Fon* and *Yoruba* origin, ethnic groups from Dahomey (now Benin) and Nigeria respectively, began to organize themselves into structured communities in Bahia. The African priests re-established their places of worship—the sanctuaries that congregated the community of initiated believers. These slaves observed their own religions' rituals—dance, music, sacrifices and offerings that up to that time had been limited by their masters. Much of the daily food of both slaves and what was prepared for the deities was recreated during this period. The African gods were believed to eat what humans eat, and then, as today, more elaborate foods were prepared for religious feasts and votive celebrations.

Slave cooks often prepared Portuguese menus, but substituted African ingredients, colored the stews with red palm oil, and invented a variety of porridge dishes using bananas and yams, boiled or fried in oil. They created new dishes with an old taste, using palm oil, hot peppers and okra that enabled them to maintain and preserve the diet of the African deities. Thus, the African gods, called *orixás*, were able to eat their favorite foods in Brazil, in Bahia as well as in Pernambuco, Rio, and elsewhere.

Apart from its use in *Candomblé* and *Macumba*, as the religion is known in Rio, this markedly African cuisine is not only present in the daily fare of Brazilians, but also at folk celebrations and festivals, at lunches and dinners to celebrate birthdays, anniversaries, and other special occasions, at receptions for visitors, and at many restaurants that serve food known as "typical." This cuisine is not confined to Bahia, but has spread throughout the country from the state of Amazonas in the north to Rio Grande do Sul in the south not as a daily fare, but certainly as a cuisine that is served for special occasions.

BRAZIL'S CONTRIBUTION TO WORLD CUISINE

The Portuguese established the first empire upon which the sun never set. By virtue of Portugal's early presence in Africa, Asia, and South America, they became the first carriers of language, social norms, culture, and agricultural products to different parts of the globe. Not only were the Portuguese the first intercontinental and interregional carriers of agricultural products, they were also the purveyors of many food cultures.

Portuguese mariners introduced Amerindian, as well as African and Asian, agricultural products to many parts of the world. From Brazil they took tomatoes, potatoes, peppers, avocados, chocolate, manioc, and guaraná, a drink made by the Maués Indians from the powdered seeds of the *cipó* tree that grows in the Amazon forest. The Portuguese also took the sweet potato from its native South America to Africa. From Africa the sweet potato spread to Europe, North America, and Asia. Another fascinating example is that of the peanut. This legume, native to South America, traveled in the cargo of Portuguese merchant ships to Africa. African slaves then brought it back across the Atlantic and introduced it in North America. As a matter of fact, in Kimbundu, a Bantu language of Angola, the word for peanut is *nguba*. In the U.S., especially in the south, "goober" is a peanut.

Okra, a vegetable native to Africa was taken by the Portuguese to Brazil. Indeed, okra, and *quiabo*, the Portuguese equivalent, as well as *gumbo*, are all words of West African origin. When okra was introduced to Brazil, it resembled a local thick-leaf plant called *caruru* by the Tupi-Guarani Indians. And, indeed, okra is the main ingredient of a now classic Afro-Brazilian dish first concocted in Bahia. This stew-like shrimp and okra dish is known, however, as *caruru*. The story does not end there. *Caruru* was taken to Africa by the Portuguese and became a part of Angolan cuisine. Contract workers, known as *angolares*, took the dish to the islands of São Tomé and Príncipe, a former Portuguese colony in the Gulf of Guinea. There the original Tupi word was modified to *calulu*, the name of a much loved chicken and okra dish. Finally, the Brazilian Indian word, spelled *calalu*, *kalulu*, or *callaloo*, emigrated to Jamaica and to Louisiana as the names of a variety of leafy greens used in creole cooking, particularly soups. Whatever the word, its orthographic variants, and the dishes to which it refers, the Portuguese, and Brazilians, were the original propagators.

Portuguese mariners were also responsible for the initial dissemination of one of the world's best known and most appreciated cereal crops. That grass plant is, of course, corn, a crop that North American, Caribbean, and Brazilian Indians cultivated long before the arrival of Europeans. *Milho*, the Portuguese word for corn, was introduced to Europe and Africa in the early seventeenth century by the Portuguese.

The recipes in this cookbook include the foods native to Brazil and the foods that colonizers, slaves, and immigrants brought to this land. All of those foods resulted in what is known today as traditional Brazilian cuisine.

Northern Cuisine

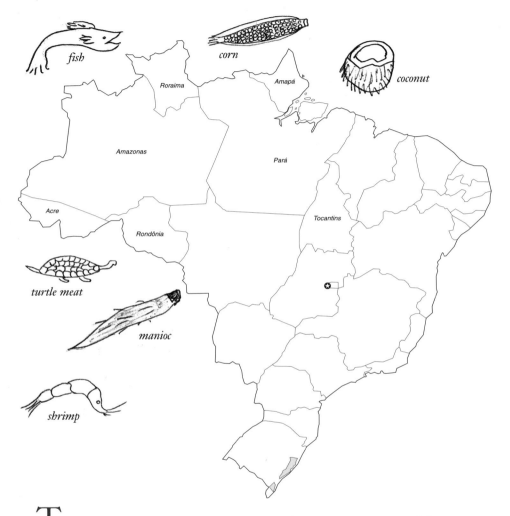

The northern region of Brazil occupies almost sixty percent of the country and includes the states of Amazonas, Pará, and Acre and the territories of Amapá, Rondônia, Roraima, and Tocantins. When the first Europeans arrived around 1530 there were approximately six hundred Indian nations in the Amazon region alone. They were very diverse in culture, ethnicity, and language and even foodways. For the next two hundred years, the Europeans were confronted by their own need to acculturate and adapt to certain indigenous customs. Many abandoned their European clothing (not appropriate in the heat of the tropics) and adopted native attire. A horrified sixteenth-century

Portuguese clergyman testified that many of the settlers only dressed in western fashion when they had to attend to important matters. Prior to the discoveries, the Portuguese diet was based on meat and fish including soups and stews. To the Portuguese, already internationalized at that time and familiar with the oriental palate's strong aromatic seasonings like cloves, cinnamon, nutmeg, fresh and dried pepper—food found in Brazil was relatively bland. More than an encounter, it was a confrontation between indigenous cooking and the European way of eating and drinking. The Portuguese ate the rations and foods that came by ships and slowly incorporated fish, fruit, smoked game and roots.

By the mid seventeenth century only traces of the Portuguese cuisine remained; the food of the region was largely indigenous consisting mainly of fish, game, and seasonal fruits. Many of the colonizers also enjoyed a daily glass of assay wine made from the fruit of the assay palm tree that grows on the banks of rivers or in marshy areas. By the eighteenth century the indigenous-based gastronomy was infused with contributions from Portugal, India, and Africa. Local fruits were made into jams, preserves, syrups, and candies thanks to the sugarcane plantations. The Indians, however, were faithful to their culinary customs and continued to prepare their meals in the traditional manner. They roasted meat on wooden stick skewers over a low fire or in an oven in the ground called a *biaribi*. For the latter they dug a hole, lined it with leaves on which the meat was placed, also wrapped in leaves, and poured dirt over all. They lit fires over the dirt and kept them going until the meat was cooked.

Another staple of the Indian diet was ground manioc. It accompanied almost every meal either as a side dish or mixed with meat or fish. Manioc meal was slowly incorporated into the Portuguese and African diets. The Portuguese began to use manioc meal to thicken meat and fish broths and the African slaves began to make *pirão* (a porridge made with broth). Tapioca is also a byproduct of manioc meal. It was enriched with coconut milk, cinnamon, and sugar, an Arabic custom that the Portuguese assimilated and disseminated.

Guarana, a fruit from the Amazon, has long been a part of the indigenous diet. Today it is made into a sparkling beverage that is widely enjoyed throughout Brazil. The process involved in making this drink is attributed to the Maue Indians. They dried the pulp of the fruit in the sun and then shaped it into sticks. The sticks were then grated using the rough tongue of the large pirarucu fish. This product was then mixed with water to make a drink. The Indians carried this beverage with them when they went hunting. It was said to give them such energy that they could go from one day to another and not feel hungry.

The waters of the Amazon and the San Francisco rivers are home to many types of fish, the best known of which is the pirarucu. This freshwater fish can reach seven feet in length and weighs between 100 and 150 pounds. Once caught, the fish is cut into pieces of about forty pounds each, salted and sent to market. Pirarucu is an indigenous word meaning "red fish," *urucu* being the name of a native red fruit. This fruit had many uses for the Indians. In addition to its culinary purpose, they extracted the pigment to use for body paintings and decorative applications for pottery and woven cloth.

In addition to the various types of fish found in the rivers and oceans, one of the regional foods that is enjoyed by all social classes is turtle meat. Family lunches often include *tartarugada*, a popular turtle stew served in its shell with a *farofa* (manioc meal sautéed with turtle eggs).

In the early days, local fishermen and farmers sold their wares from makeshift stands. Today we find marketplaces with stalls of fish, vegetables, flours, and cereals, a special area for artifacts woven from natural fibers, decorated with the dye of the *urucu*, and stalls piled high with various types of salted meat and tortoise steaks, bins of rice, and tapioca. Outside the market are stalls devoted to various spices and other seasonings, huge mounds of ground black and red pepper, cinnamon, cloves, and hot red peppers. There are also many venders selling *beijus*, thin cakes made from tapioca flour, to hungry shoppers.

The indigenous peoples of the northern region not only gave us the hammock, but also an original and traditional strain of northern Brazilian cuisine. The food is a direct extension of the Portuguese voyage of discovery and love of foods with a rich mixture of ingredients. It is the convergence of local traditions with European and African creations and contributions. It has a native indigenous base that incorporated the encounters of the European, African, and Asian worlds, nationalizing customs that predate the arrival of the Portuguese in Brazil over five hundred years ago.

Plantain Chips

Banana-Pacova em Rodelas

8 SERVINGS

THESE PLANTAIN CHIPS are popular throughout Latin America and in much of the Caribbean. In northern Brazil they are fried in soy or peanut oil and served as an appetizer or as an accompaniment to *Feijoada Baiana* (page 54). In the Amazon region these plantain chips are served with ice-cold sugarcane juice.

4 CUPS SOY OR PEANUT OIL	SALT TO TASTE
4 LARGE GREEN PLANTAINS	

Heat the oil in a large deep skillet to 350°F. Peel the plantains and slice (about ¼ inch thick) directly into the hot oil using a mandoline or a sharp knife. Do not crowd the skillet; fry about 10 slices at a time. When the plantains are golden, remove the chips and drain on absorbent paper. Sprinkle with salt to taste.

Fish Balls

Bolinhos de Pirarucu
YIELDS 30 BALLS

PIRARUCU IS THE BEST KNOWN fish in the Amazon region, and this is but one of the many ways it is prepared. Since pirarucu is not available in the U.S., you can substitute any salted fish, preferably cod. These fish balls are usually served as an appetizer with pepper sauce and lime slices.

2 POUNDS SALTED PIRARUCU OR SALT COD	1 TABLESPOON CHOPPED FRESH CILANTRO
2 POUNDS MANIOC ROOT	1 EGG, LIGHTLY BEATEN
2 MEDIUM ONIONS, FINELY CHOPPED	1 CUP FLOUR
2 CHERRY PEPPERS, FINELY CHOPPED	4 CUPS VEGETABLE OIL
1 BANANA PEPPER, FINELY CHOPPED	

Cover the salted fish with cold water and refrigerate for at least 12 hours, changing the water at least 4 times. Peel the manioc root, cut into chunks and boil until tender, about 20 minutes. Remove the center core from the manioc and mash it or put through a ricer. Flake the fish, removing any skin and bones and add it to the mashed manioc. Add the onion, banana and cherry peppers, cilantro, egg, and 2 tablespoons of the flour. Mix well and form into balls the size of walnuts. Heat the oil in a deep skillet to 350°F. Roll the fish balls in the remaining flour and fry about 6 at a time until golden.

Serve warm with hot pepper sauce and lime slices.

Fried Fish Cubes *with* Garden Sauce

Iscas de Pirarucu ao Molho Floresta
MAKES 30 CUBES

IN THE AMAZON REGION the preferred fish for this recipe is pirarucu. Since it is not available outside of Brazil, fresh cod or haddock can be substituted with good results. This appetizer is usually served on toothpicks with Garden Sauce (recipe follows) for dipping.

FISH:	GARDEN SAUCE: (MAKES 2 CUPS)
2 POUNDS BONELESS FISH FILLETS (COD, HADDOCK, OR OTHER WHITE FISH)	1 MEDIUM ONION, MINCED
	1 SMALL HOT PEPPER, SEEDED
	¼ CUP LIME JUICE
3 LIMES, HALVED	1 GREEN BELL PEPPER, SEEDED AND CHOPPED
1 TEASPOON SALT	
¼ CUP LEMON JUICE	5 CHERRY PEPPERS, CHOPPED
1 CUP FLOUR FOR DREDGING	1 BUNCH PARSLEY, CHOPPED
VEGETABLE OIL FOR FRYING	2 TEASPOONS WHITE VINEGAR
	1 CUP OLIVE OIL

FOR THE FISH: Rub the fish with the cut limes. Cut the fillets into 1-inch cubes and season with the salt and lemon juice. Place in the refrigerator for 20 minutes. Pat the fish dry with a paper towel and roll in the flour to coat, shaking off excess flour. Set aside. Pour 2 inches of oil into a deep skillet. Heat the oil to 350°F and fry the cubes until golden. Drain on paper towels. Skewer each cube with a toothpick and place on a serving tray. Serve with garden sauce.

FOR THE SAUCE: Place all the ingredients in a blender and pulse until a thick sauce forms. If it is too thick add a little water.

NOTE: This sauce is also a great accompaniment for other fried appetizers such as croquettes, fritters and pastries.

Shrimp Omelet

Omelete de Aviú

2 SERVINGS

AVIÚS ARE TINY FRESH water shrimp native to the Amazon region. When grilled or fried they can be eaten without peeling. In this recipe small shrimp are layered between beaten eggs. Serve this omelet for brunch or a light supper with a green salad and sliced papaya or melon.

1 POUND SMALL FRESH SHRIMP, PEELED, DEVEINED, AND HALVED	2 GREEN ONIONS, CHOPPED
JUICE OF 3 LIMES	1 TOMATO, PEELED, SEEDED, AND CHOPPED
¼ CUP OLIVE OIL	2 CHERRY PEPPERS, CHOPPED
¼ CUP CHOPPED FRESH PARSLEY	6 EGGS, SEPARATED
¼ CUP CHOPPED FRESH CILANTRO	

Marinate the shrimp in the lime juice for 30 minutes. Drain.

Heat 1 tablespoon of the olive oil in a medium skillet over medium heat and sauté the parsley, cilantro, green onions, tomatoes, and cherry peppers. Add the shrimp and cook, stirring, until no longer pink.

In a large bowl, beat the egg whites until stiff. Lightly beat the egg yolks and add them 1 at a time, folding gently. Heat the remaining 3 tablespoons of oil in a 10-inch skillet. Pour in half of the eggs, tilting to spread evenly over the pan and cook for 1 minute. Place the shrimp mixture over the eggs and cover with the remaining eggs. Lower the heat, cover the skillet, and cook for 2 minutes. Uncover and using a metal spatula, slide the omelet onto a large plate. Place the skillet over the plate and flip the omelet back into the pan to cook the other side. When the underside is done, place on a platter and cut into 6 to 8 wedges. Serve with a green salad.

NOTE: If you use an ovenproof skillet, place the pan under the broiler instead of flipping it.

Shrimp *and* Brazil Nut Soup

Crème de Camarão ao Leite de Castanha

12 SERVINGS

THIS IS A DELICIOUS version of the Catalan almond soup made with Brazil nuts. The Portuguese brought this shrimp dish to the Americas where the Brazil nut was added. When fresh, Brazil nuts can be ground and pressed to produce milk. The combination of the milk with manioc flour is a delicious addition.

4 TOMATOES, PEELED AND SEEDED	2 TEASPOONS SALT
2 ONIONS, 1 CHOPPED AND 1 GRATED	1 TABLESPOON BUTTER
1 GREEN BELL PEPPER, CHOPPED	3 QUARTS SKIM MILK
¼ CUP OLIVE OIL	3 CUPS MANIOC MEAL (TAPIOCA FLOUR)
4 GARLIC CLOVES, CRUSHED	2 CUPS BRAZIL NUT MILK (SEE NOTE)
2 POUNDS SHRIMP, PEELED AND DEVEINED	1 CUP GRATED ASIAGO CHEESE
1 BOUQUET GARNI	

Place the tomatoes, chopped onion, and green pepper in the blender, process thoroughly and set aside. Heat a skillet and add the olive oil. Add the garlic and cook until lightly golden. Add the shrimp, the tomato mixture, the bouquet garni, and salt, stirring for about 5 minutes or until the shrimp turn pink. Remove from the heat and set aside.

In another large skillet, heat the butter. Add the grated onions and brown lightly. Add the milk and bring to a boil. Add the shrimp mixture and tapioca flour stirring constantly until it thickens and the tapioca is soft. Remove the pan from the heat and let stand for about 5 minutes. Slowly add the Brazil nut milk stirring constantly to keep the mixture from curdling. Serve hot sprinkled with grated cheese.

NOTE: To make Brazil nut milk place 3 cups of chopped Brazil nuts into a blender with ½ cup water and blend on high until the mixture resembles a purée. Place the mixture in a cheesecloth and squeeze to extract all the liquid. If the milk gets too thick, add hot milk a little at a time, stirring constantly (Chopping the nuts before blending makes it easier for the blender to grind to a powder).

Crab Soup

Sopa de Caranguejo
4 SERVINGS

CRABS ABOUND ALONG the coast of Brazil, and there are many wonderful dishes that use this delicious crustacean. This soup, which incorporates crab with coconut milk, palm oil, and vegetables, offers an unusual combination of ingredients that will tickle your palate.

2 POUNDS CRABMEAT	1 (15-OUNCE) CAN GREEN PEAS,
4 LIMES, HALVED	DRAINED OR 1 (10-OUNCE) PACKAGE
2 TABLESPOONS PALM OIL	FROZEN PEAS
1 BUNCH PARSLEY, CHOPPED	1 BUNCH CILANTRO, CHOPPED
1 BUNCH GREEN ONIONS, CHOPPED	2 CUPS COCONUT MILK
1 LARGE ONION, CHOPPED	1 CUP OLIVE OIL
2 TOMATOES, PEELED AND CHOPPED	2 CUPS MANIOC FLOUR
2 BAKING POTATOES, PEELED AND	
CHOPPED	

Place the crab in a strainer set over a bowl, squeeze the limes over the crabmeat and let stand in the refrigerator for about 5 minutes. Rinse the crabmeat quickly and drain.

Heat the palm oil in a large skillet and sauté the crabmeat with the parsley, green onions, onions, tomatoes, potatoes, peas, and cilantro.

In another skillet heat the coconut milk and olive oil and add the crab mixture. Slowly pour the manioc flour into the mixture, stirring constantly until the soup thickens and has a smooth consistency. Serve hot.

NOTE: If the soup is too thick, add a little more coconut milk.

Cassava Leaf *and* Meat Medley

Maniçoba

4 SERVINGS

MANIÇOBA IS ONE OF THE MOST POPULAR dishes of the states of Amazona and Pará. It is also very popular in the city of Cachoeira, on the Bay of Bahia, where cooks also add a bit of pig stomach. In Brazil the leaves of the cassava plant are used, but, because they contain cyanic acid, they have to be cooked for 7 days before they can be eaten. A good substitute is pumpkin leaves or spinach, which does not greatly alter the taste.

1 POUND SPINACH OR PUMPKIN LEAVES, STEMMED	⅓ CUP LARD OR SHORTENING
	1 BAY LEAF
1 POUND DRIED BEEF, SOAKED OVERNIGHT	4 GARLIC CLOVES, MINCED
	1 ONION, MINCED
½ POUND STEWING BEEF, CUBED	1 TABLESPOON CHOPPED FRESH MINT
¼ POUND SALT PORK, CUBED	½ TEASPOON BLACK PEPPER
½ POUND PORTUGUESE SMOKED SAUSAGE, CUBED	½ TEASPOON GROUND CUMIN

Grind the spinach in a meat grinder or food processor until minced. Place the dried beef into a pot, cover with water and bring to a boil. Then reduce the heat and simmer for 10 minutes. In a separate pot place the stewing beef, salt pork, and sausage. Cover with water, bring to a boil, reduce the heat and simmer for 10 minutes. Add the spinach and cook for 4 hours over low heat or until the meats are tender.

Meanwhile, melt the lard in a large skillet and sauté the bay leaf, garlic, onion, mint, pepper, and cumin until the onion is translucent. When the meats are tender, add the onion mixture. Mix well and serve with white or brown rice.

Banana Tacate

Tacate

4 SERVINGS

THE ORIGINAL *TACATE* is indigenous to the Amazon region. To prepare the dish the Indians used a local fish mixed with bananas and served it in banana leaves. The Portuguese prepared this Indian dish with sausage instead of fish. The assimilated version later became a popular dish of the northern region.

---

10 GREEN PLANTAINS
SALT TO TASTE
½ POUND FRESH PORTUGUESE
  SAUSAGE LINKS

2 TABLESPOONS OLIVE OIL

Peel the plantains and then cut them into 1-inch slices. Place in a medium-size pot and barely cover with water. Add salt to taste and cook until soft, about 15 minutes. Drain and mince the plantain. Slice the sausage links into 1-inch pieces. Heat the olive oil in a skillet and add the sausages. Cook for about 20 minutes, turning frequently, until the sausages are brown on all sides. Mix the sausage slices with the plantain pieces. Serve warm.

NOTE: Some cooks remove the sausage from its casing and sauté it, breaking it up like ground beef. It is then mixed with the plantains, rolled up in a banana leaf, and baked. If banana leaves are unavailable, use corn husks.

Barbecued Fish *with* Bean Salad *and* Jambu Rice

Filhote Pai-d' égua
12 SERVINGS

THIS DELICIOUS FISH DISH is usually reserved for lunch on Sundays or for special dinners because of the time it takes to prepare. It is particularly popular in the city of Belém in the state of Pará where *filhote* fish abound in the Amazon River.

6 POUNDS FIRM WHITE FISH FILLETS (GROUPER, SNAPPER, COD, OR HADDOCK)	¼ CUP OLIVE OIL
	8 SMALL ONIONS, QUARTERED
	5 GREEN BELL PEPPERS, CUT INTO EIGHTHS
JUICE OF 5 LIMES	8 MEDIUM TOMATOES, CUT INTO WEDGES OR 32 CHERRY TOMATOES
5 GARLIC CLOVES, CHOPPED	
½ CUP WHITE WINE VINEGAR	FLOUR FOR DREDGING
2 CUPS WHITE WINE	
2 TEASPOONS SALT	

Cut the fish into 2-inch cubes. Rinse with cold water and the juice of 2 of the limes; pat dry. Place the fish in a large bowl and prepare a marinade with the juice of the remaining 3 limes, the garlic, vinegar, wine, salt, and olive oil. Marinate the fish for at least 6 hours, refrigerated.

Heat coals until white or a gas grill until hot. If using a gas grill, lightly oil it. Drain the fish and pat dry. Place 4 fish cubes on each skewer alternating with a tomato wedge, onion wedge, and a green pepper wedge. Dust the kebobs lightly with flour, shaking to remove any excess, and place over hot coals. Turn occasionally until browned all over.

To serve, place the kabobs on individual plates with butterbean salad on one side and a small mold of *jambu* rice on the other. Use slices of tomatoes, onions, and bell peppers to decorate the plate, topping the fish and bean salad (recipes follow).

Butterbean Salad

Salada de Feijão Manteiga

12 SERVINGS

1 POUND BUTTERBEANS	5 GREEN ONIONS, CHOPPED
3 TOMATOES, PEELED AND MINCED	JUICE OF 2 LIMES
3 ONIONS, MINCED	½ CUP WHITE WINE VINEGAR
2 GREEN BELL PEPPERS, MINCED	1 TEASPOON SALT
3 GARLIC CLOVES, MINCED	¼ CUP OLIVE OIL
1 CHERRY PEPPER, CHOPPED	3 SLICES BACON, COOKED AND
2 TABLESPOONS CHOPPED FRESH	CRUMBLED
PARSLEY	

Shell the beans, wash and place in a pot with water to cover. Bring to a boil, reduce the heat and simmer for 20 minutes or until the beans are al dente. Drain and let cool.

In a large bowl, mix together the tomatoes, onions, bell peppers, garlic, cherry pepper, parsley, green onions, lime juice, vinegar, salt, olive oil, and 2 to 3 tablespoons water. Add the vinaigrette and bacon to the beans and mix well.

Jambu Rice

Arroz de Jambu

12 SERVINGS

JAMBU IS AN EDIBLE PLANT from the Amazon region that is also found in India. It is also known as *agrião-do-Pará* and is related to the nasturtium family. The leaves are similar to watercress in taste and texture. I have substituted watercress in this recipe with great results.

1 TEASPOON SALT	¼ CUP OLIVE OIL
1 BUNCH WATERCRESS	2 GARLIC CLOVES, THINLY SLICED
2 CUPS WHITE RICE	⅓ ONION, MINCED

Bring 6 cups of water to a boil with the salt in a 2-quart saucepan. Chop the watercress into ½-inch pieces and add it to the boiling water. When the water returns to a boil, cook for 3 minutes. Remove the watercress and reserve 4 cups of the water. Cook the rice in the reserved water. Heat the olive oil in a skillet and sauté the garlic and onion until golden. Add the watercress and cooked rice. Taste for salt, mix well, and serve.

Pará-Style Shrimp Pudding

Vatapá Paraense
10 SERVINGS

THE MONTH OF JUNE is one of the most festive months of the year in the North, especially the celebration of St. John's Day and St. Anthony's Day. A popular dish served during these festivities is *vatapá*, one of the best known Afro-Brazilian dishes in the North and Northeast of Brazil. In the North, *vatapá* is made with flour and in the Northeast it is made with bread. In the state of Pará they also add tomatoes, parsley, green onions, and olive oil, while in the state of Bahia, cashews, peanuts, and fresh fish are added. This version is from the state of Pará.

½ POUND DRIED SHRIMP	3 CUPS FLOUR
1 POUND FRESH SHRIMP	2 TABLESPOONS OLIVE OIL
2 MEDIUM ONIONS, DICED	¼ CUP PALM OIL
2 MEDIUM TOMATOES, DICED	2 CUPS COCONUT MILK
1 TABLESPOON MINCED FRESH PARSLEY	2 SMALL RED HOT PEPPERS
1 TABLESPOON MINCED GREEN ONION	JUICE OF 2 LEMONS

Rinse the dried shrimp and soak it for 1 hour in warm water. Drain and place the shrimp in a saucepan with 3 cups of water. Bring to a boil and cook for 5 minutes. Drain and reserve the broth. In a meat grinder or food processor grind the dried shrimp.

Heat the olive oil in a large skillet. Add the fresh shrimp, ground shrimp, onions, tomatoes, parsley, and green onions. Mix well and sauté the mixture for 2 minutes. Add the flour ½ cup at a time, stirring constantly until well blended. Slowly add the palm oil and the coconut milk, stirring constantly until well blended. Cook for an additional 15 minutes or until it resembles a thick purée. If it is too thick, add a little more coconut milk

Serve with white or brown rice.

Stuffed Crab *in its* Shell

Casquinha de Carangueijo
10 SERVINGS

STUFFED CRAB IN ITS SHELL is popular throughout the Portuguese-speaking world. From Macau to Brazil it's a dish that you will find served at parties and special celebrations, as well as in many restaurants. There are many variations depending on the region and local ingredients. Land crabs are used in this recipe from the Amazon.

CRAB:	FAROFA:
1 POUND LUMP CRABMEAT	⅔ CUP BUTTER OR MARGARINE
2 LIMES	4 GARLIC CLOVES, MINCED
3 TABLESPOONS OLIVE OIL	4 CUPS MANIOC FLOUR
2 MEDIUM TOMATOES, CHOPPED	
2 MEDIUM ONIONS, CHOPPED	TO SERVE:
1 BUNCH PARSLEY, CHOPPED	10 CRAB SHELLS
5 GREEN ONIONS, CHOPPED	½ CUP CHOPPED BLACK OLIVES
¼ CUP MINCED HABANERO OR OTHER	1 TABLESPOON MINCED HOT
HOT PEPPER	RED PEPPER
	1 TEASPOON SALT

FOR THE CRAB: Place the crabmeat in a colander. Squeeze the limes over the crabmeat and let stand for 10 minutes. In a large skillet, heat the olive oil and sauté the tomato, onion, parsley, green onion, and habanero pepper. Add the crabmeat and stir to combine well. Fill the crab shells with the mixture and keep warm.

FOR THE FAROFA: Melt the butter in a medium-size skillet and sauté the garlic until lightly golden. Stir in the manioc flour until it is well absorbed and the mixture resembles corn meal. Add the olives, hot pepper, and salt. Sprinkle the farofa over the stuffed shells and place under the broiler for 1 minute to brown.

Serve warm.

Tapioca Rolls

Pãezinhos de Tapioca

MAKES 30 ROLLS

QUITANDAS, ARE HOMEMADE PASTRIES, breads, biscuits, cornbread, and cakes, displayed on trays and the *quitandeira* is the maker or vender of such products. These tasty little rolls eaten at breakfast or for an afternoon snack are one example of the many baked goods produced in the north. They are a perfect combination of the Portuguese culinary technique of bread making and a New World indigenous ingredient, tapioca.

4 CUPS TAPIOCA	1 TABLESPOON BUTTER
1½ CUPS WHOLE MILK	2 TABLESPOONS SUGAR
4 EGGS	1 TEASPOON SALT

Preheat the oven to 350°F. Grease a baking sheet with butter.

Place the tapioca in a large bowl, pour the milk over the tapioca and set aside until the tapioca swells and softens, about 20 minutes. Add the eggs, 1 at a time to the tapioca, stirring after each addition. Then add the butter, sugar, and salt and mix well with a wooden spoon.

Using a tablespoon, place scoops of the batter on the baking sheet leaving 2 inches between each roll. Bake the rolls for about 20 minutes or until lightly browned. Serve hot with butter.

Pumpkin Bread

Pão de Jerimon
MAKES 1 LOAF

PUMPKIN BREAD is very popular in the states of Amazonas and Pará. It is usually served at breakfast or for an afternoon snack. If pumpkin is not available you can substitute butternut squash.

1 CUP PUMPKIN OR BUTTERNUT SQUASH PURÉE	¼ CUP SUGAR
	¼ CUP POWDERED MILK
3½ CUPS FLOUR	¼ CUP BUTTER OR MARGARINE,
2 TABLESPOONS YEAST	SOFTENED
1 EGG	1 TEASPOON SALT

Preheat the oven to 350°F. Grease a 9 x 5-inch loaf pan.

In a large bowl, mix the pumpkin, 2 cups of the flour, and the yeast. Add the egg, sugar, powdered milk, butter, salt, and ¼ cup water. Mix well. Add more water as necessary if the dough is too stiff. Place on lightly floured surface and knead for about 5 minutes until dough is smooth and elastic. Pour into the prepared pan, cover and let rise for 50 minutes until double in volume.

Bake 50 to 60 minutes or until a toothpick inserted in the center comes out clean. Turn out onto a rack and cool.

NOTE: This bread will keep well wrapped in the refrigerator for a week.

Well-Married Cookies

Casadinhos

MAKES 75 COOKIES

DUE TO THE LACK OF COWS and hence, cow's milk in the north of Brazil, people have used canned condensed milk in their cooking, especially in desserts, since the beginning of the nineteenth century. This was not the case in the rest of Brazil where cows were common.

These cookies, popular in the cities of Manaus and Belém, are an example of the use of condensed milk for desserts.

WHITE DOUGH:	CHOCOLATE DOUGH:
1 TABLESPOON BUTTER	1 TABLESPOON BUTTER
2 (14-OUNCE) CANS SWEETENED CONDENSED MILK	¼ CUP COCOA POWDER
	2 (14-OUNCE) CANS CONDENSED MILK
	POWDERED SUGAR

FOR THE WHITE DOUGH: Place the butter and condensed milk in a heavy pot over low heat. Stir constantly until the mixture thickens and pulls away from the sides of the pan, about 20 minutes. Transfer to a buttered plate and cool.

FOR THE CHOCOLATE DOUGH: Place the butter, cocoa powder, and condensed milk in a pot over low heat and follow the same procedure as for the white dough.

Roll out each batch of dough and cut into 3-inch strips or circles. Place a white piece of dough over a chocolate one and roll in powdered sugar. Place in fluted cups or on a serving tray.

Banana Brittle

Pé-de-Moleque de Banana-Pacova
MAKES 50 PIECES

PÉ-DE-MOLEQUE IS A VERY POPULAR candy in the northeast of Brazil made with peanuts and cooked on top of the stove. In the Amazon region it is prepared with manioc root and plantains and baked in banana leaves in the oven. Both versions are delicious. The term *moleque*, meaning "boy," comes from the Angolan Kimbundu language. In Brazilian Portuguese, *moleque* means "urchin" or "brat" and the Portuguese word *pê* translates as foot. Thus, the literal translation of the candy's name is "urchin's foot." For this recipe, instead of banana leaves, you can use aluminum foil.

4 POUNDS MANIOC ROOT	4 CUPS SUGAR
2 POUNDS RIPE PLANTAINS, MASHED	1 TABLESPOON ANISEED
4 CUPS BRAZIL NUTS, CHOPPED (16 OUNCES)	1 TEASPOON GROUND CLOVES

Preheat the oven to 350°F.

Peel and grate the manioc, removing the center core and place it in a plastic bag. Add the mashed plantains, Brazil nuts, sugar, aniseed, and cloves. Knead the mixture until a smooth dough forms. Spread the dough out on the counter or a cutting board and cut into 2-inch squares. Cut squares out of aluminum foil large enough to form a packet holding each square. Place the packets on a cookie sheet and bake for 40 minutes. Unwrap, cool, and place on a serving tray.

NOTE: Will keep at room temperature for 1 week in an air-tight container or for 2 weeks in the refrigerator.

Coconut *and* Plantain Candy

Cocada com Banana-Pacova

24 SQUARES

COCADA, OR COCONUT CANDY, is very popular in Brazil as well as Angola. In Brazil it is sold by *Baianas* (women in white lace dresses who belong to the Afro-Brazilian religious cult *Candomblé*) on street corners as well as in bakeries. In Angola it is sprinkled with cinnamon and sold in one solid piece while in Brazil it is broken into squares after it hardens and sold by the piece. In the Northern region of Brazil it is customary to add plantains to the candy. *Cocada* is usually served at parties and for religious holidays.

1 CUP GRATED COCONUT (FROZEN OR FRESH)	2 RIPE PLANTAINS, MASHED
1 (14 OUNCE) CAN SWEETENED CONDENSED MILK	4 CUPS SUGAR

In a large pot cook the coconut, condensed milk, mashed plantains, and sugar over medium heat, stirring until the mixture caramelizes and comes away from the sides of the pan. Pour onto a buttered surface, spread ½ inch thick and let cool. Cut into squares with a sharp knife.

NOTE: These candies keep for several weeks in an airtight container.

Brazil Nut Torte

Torta de Castanha-do-Pará

8 TO 10 SERVINGS

BRAZIL NUTS, also known as Pará nuts, after the name of the state, and originally called *nhá*, in the region, are highly appreciated in the Amazon and exported to many countries around the world. One Brazil nut tree is able to produce as much as 1,000 pounds of nuts a year. This recipe is another example of the versatility of the Brazil nut in Brazilian cuisine.

3¼ CUPS SUGAR	1 TEASPOON BAKING POWDER
5 STICKS BUTTER, SOFTENED	1½ CUPS CANNED PRUNES IN SYRUP,
8 EGGS, SEPARATED	DRAINED (8 OUNCES)
2½ CUPS BRAZIL NUTS, FINELY	1 (14-OUNCE) CAN CONDENSED MILK
CHOPPED	BOILED (SEE NOTE)
3 CUPS FLOUR	½ CUP MUSCATEL WINE

Preheat the oven to 350°F and grease two 10-inch cake pans.

Whisk together 2 cups of the sugar and 4 sticks of the butter until creamy. Add the yolks, one at a time, beating until well blended. Add ½ cup of the Brazil nuts, the flour, and baking powder. Beat the egg whites until stiff peaks form and fold into the batter. Pour the batter into the prepared pans. Bake for 30 minutes or until the torte springs back when lightly touched. Cool in the pans on cake racks for 10 minutes, then loosen the sides and turn out onto racks to cool.

FOR THE FILLING: Place the prunes in a blender with the boiled condensed milk and wine. Blend to a thick purée. Slice the cake in half and spread with the filling.

TO PREPARE THE ICING: Beat the remaining sugar and butter until creamy. Mix in ¾ cup of the remaining Brazil nuts. Cover the top and sides of the cake with the icing. Decorate the top of the torte with the remaining ¾ cup nuts.

NOTE: To boil condensed milk, pour into a small pot and bring to a boil. Reduce the heat and, stirring constantly, cook for 5 minutes. Let cool.

Tapioca Pudding

Pudim de Tapioca

8 SERVINGS

THIS TAPIOCA PUDDING is not the same as the pudding we know and love in the U.S. *Pudim de tapioca* is a typical dessert of the northern region. It is a by-product of the manioc root and can be prepared two ways; with a caramel coating similar to a flan or covered with meringue. This recipe from the state of Amazonas has a caramel coating.

1½ CUPS TAPIOCA FLOUR	1 TABLESPOON BUTTER, SOFTENED
1 CUP COCONUT MILK	1 (14-OUNCE) CAN SWEETENED
1½ CUPS SUGAR	CONDENSED MILK
5 EGGS	1 CUP HEAVY CREAM

Place the tapioca flour in a bowl with the coconut milk and soak for 1 hour.

Preheat the oven to 350°F.

Heat the sugar slowly in a heavy skillet, stirring constantly with a wooden spoon until it melts and is free of lumps. When the sugar turns a caramel color, remove from the heat and pour into an 8-cup ovenproof dish. Set aside to harden for 5 minutes. Fill a pan, large enough to hold the pudding dish with 1 inch of hot water to create a bain-marie.

Beat the eggs in a large bowl until frothy. Add the butter, condensed milk, and cream, mixing continuously. Add the tapioca mixture to the egg mixture.

Pour the pudding into the dish and place in the pan of hot water. Bake for 40 minutes or until a toothpick inserted into the pudding comes out clean.

Amazon Ginger Ale

Aluá de Milho
MAKES 1 GALLON

THE PEOPLE OF THE AMAZON region use many native fruits and vegetables to make drinks. This popular beverage is made from roasted corn and is similar to what we call ginger ale.

5 POUNDS CORN ON THE COB	4 POUNDS BROWN SUGAR
1 POUND FRESH GINGER	

Soak the ears of corn in their husks for 1 hour. Roast the corn over hot coals, turning, until it is cooked, about 20 minutes. Shuck the corn and slice the kernels from the cob with a sharp knife. Place the corn in an earthenware pot with 4 quarts water. Cover and let sit for 3 days at room temperature. Peel and grate the ginger and add to the corn. Cover and let stand for another 5 days at room temperature. Strain the mixture through muslin and then sweeten to taste with the brown sugar.

Chill the mixture and serve cold.

Northeastern Cuisine

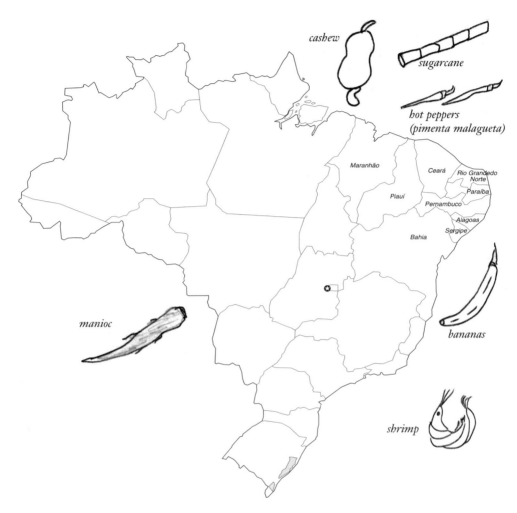

cashew

sugarcane

hot peppers
(pimenta malagueta)

Maranhão

Ceará

Rio Grande do Norte

Piauí

Paraíba

Pernambuco

Alagoas

Sergipe

Bahia

manioc

bananas

shrimp

The Brazilian Northeast encompasses the following nine states in the order of their north to south location: Maranhão, Piauí, Ceará, Rio Grande do Norte, Paraíba, Pernambuco, Alagoas, Sergipe, and Bahia. But culinary traditions are divided more by geographical areas than states and can be grouped into three main regions; the coast, the sertão, and the Bahia hinterlands. The fabulous cuisine of the northeast region results from the fusion of the culinary culture of Portuguese colonizers, native Indians, and African slaves. The Northeast, especially Bahia, had the largest influx of slaves brought in to work the sugar plantations. The result was a major African influence on the cuisine.

These food cultures reflect traditions and regional customs, and they maintained the integrity of each group from one generation to the next. One of the indigenous staples of the diet is manioc or cassava. It comes in various forms: flour, meal, tapioca and manioc leaves that are used for the dish *maniçoba*. Other typical food products are beans, corn, rice, sugarcane, shellfish, fish, and dried beef. Fruits include cashew (a fruit whose seed is known as the cashew nut), breadfruit, passion fruit, tamarind, strawberry guava, sugar apple, and many others not commonly found in North America. Curd cheese accompanies many of these fruits and the desserts prepared with them.

There is a common identity that distinguishes the Northeast from the other regions of Brazil. The different dialects, religions, and festivities, many of which are spiritual in nature, either in honor of Catholic saints or the African deities known as *orixás*, a word of Nigerian origin. Indigenous, African, Portuguese, and Asian cuisines, all come together to transform the local ingredients, enriched with products imported from overseas and products used by the slaves, such as palm oil and the malagueta pepper, to alter traditional recipes as well as create new ones. This ethnic and culinary mixing provided the flavors and tastes that make the Northeast a very special culinary region.

Sugar, which was cultivated for thousands of years in Southeast Asia, was brought to Brazil by the Portuguese. The first sugarcane plantation was established in Pernambuco in 1534 and opened the way for many other plantations throughout the Northeast. With sugarcane also came a fine confectionary tradition, including wonderful cakes and other desserts. Many of the recipes were brought by Portuguese nuns who had created them in the convents of Portugal. This baking tradition has earned the region a reputation for its confections. The more famous ones are the St. Bartolomeu cake, husband-fattening cake, Souza Leon cake, and Pernambuco basin cake. There are also preserves made from fruits, such as pumpkin, jackfruit, strawberry guava, and lime, as well as orange compote. Another by-product of sugarcane is *cachaça*, a type of brandy distilled from sugarcane juice. *Cachaça* is often translated as "white rum," although the latter is actually distilled from molasses. This very Brazilian liquor is usually served in a shot glass or in cocktails known as *batidas* and *caipirinhas*.

The cashew, an important crop, is also a common theme in much of the Northeast. It is depicted in woodcarvings, pottery, embroidery, and paintings. The fruit is dried in the sun and made into wine, juice, ice cream, and used in stews while still green. The seed, the cashew nut, grows on the outside of the fruit, and is roasted and salted. Members of the native population dried the fruit in the sun, ground it into flour, and then mixed it with roasted cashew nuts to carry as food during migrations. From the Northeast the Portuguese took the cashew to Angola, Guinea-Bissau and Mozambique in Africa, and also to India.

Dishes made with fresh shrimp and fish cooked in coconut milk are found in most of the Northeastern coastal towns and include such ingredients as palm oil, okra, coconut, and malagueta peppers. Seafood is an endless source of inspiration for new dishes, while still maintaining the traditional recipes, some from the former Portuguese colonies in Africa and Asia. Shrimp is prepared fresh, dried, or smoked, and served in pastries, soups, and stews. In Maranhão, spicy shrimp is the main ingredient in dishes that are served with corn cakes. In Ceará the famous local dish is *baião-de-dois*, made with a mixture of rice, kidney beans and curd cheese. The name baião comes from a popular musical genre that uses a trio of instruments – the triangle, the bass drum (*zabumba*), and the accordion.

In Pernambuco, cakes like Souza Leão and Roll cake are traditional specialties as is a banana preserve whose name translates as "hooker's delight" because it was known to be a favorite among prostitutes. Another treat is fried curd cheese served with sugarcane syrup and bananas sprinkled with an Arabian touch of sugar and cinnamon.

The cuisine of the Northeast reflects its people. A cuisine that bears the mark of the history of the nation to which it belongs. The Northeast is an ethnic melting pot that includes African customs, the indigenous cassava culture; the Portuguese cod, olive oil and potatoes; and the Arab spices, all forming a collection of flavors that has been labeled Northeastern.

Pepper *and* Lemon Sauce

Molho de Pimenta e Limão
MAKES 1½ CUPS

THIS SAUCE IS SERVED as an accompaniment to many Bahian dishes whether beef, pork, poultry, fish, or shellfish. It is always prepared with malagueta peppers. The green, unripe pepper is preferred. When it turns red it is less acid and less piquant. For best results, grind the peppers in a mortar and pestle.

8 TO 10 GREEN MALAGUETA OR OTHER (1- TO 2-INCH) CHILI PEPPERS	1 BUNCH PARSLEY, STEMMED
	1 BUNCH CILANTRO, STEMMED
	JUICE OF 1 LEMON
1 TEASPOON SALT	2 ONIONS, SLICED PAPER THIN

Cut the peppers in half lengthwise and remove the seeds. Place the peppers, salt, parsley, cilantro, and lemon juice in a mortar or food processor and purée. Arrange the onion slices on a dish and pour the sauce on top.

NOTE: I occasionally mix 2 tablespoons of olive oil with the purée before pouring it over the onions, which results in a smoother and tastier sauce.

Toasted Manioc Meal
with Palm Oil

Farofa de Azeite-de-Dendem
8 TO 10 SERVINGS

THE WIDELY USED *farinha de mandioca* is derived from the manioc root. *Farinha de mandioca* serves as the principal ingredient in many condiments, such as *farofas* and *pirões*. *Farofa* is lightly toasted manioc flour or meal. Frying manioc meal in palm oil is one of the many ways to prepare a *farofa*. It can also be made with water, broth, or butter. Some variations call for pumpkin, bacon, egg, or sausage. Serve this dish with Bahian Bean Stew (page 54), Pernambuco-Style Fish Steaks (page 58), or Maranhão-Style Shrimp and Okra (page 62).

2 CUPS MANIOC MEAL	¼ CUP CHOPPED BLACK OLIVES
¼ CUP PALM OIL	(OPTIONAL)
1 LARGE ONION, MINCED	
2 EGGS, HARD-BOILED AND CHOPPED	
(OPTIONAL)	

Heat a large skillet over medium heat and pour in the manioc meal. Stir constantly until the manioc is lightly toasted, then place it in a bowl. Heat the palm oil in the skillet and add the onion. Sauté the onion until it is golden. Return the manioc meal to the skillet and stir to coat completely. Serve hot or at room temperature. Garnish with hard-boiled eggs or olives.

NOTE: To serve with fish or shellfish, add ¼ pound of chopped dried or fresh shrimp to the pan with the onion, and sauté until both are golden. If using dried shrimp, soak in warm water for 20 minutes before adding them to the pan.

Black-Eyed Pea Fritters

Acarajé
MAKES 60 FRITTERS

IN BAHIA, NO PARTY IS COMPLETE without the famous *acarajé*, an appetizer made from skinless black-eyed peas and dried shrimp, fried in palm oil. *Acarajé* are usually wrapped in a piece of green or pink absorbent paper and eaten between meals, standing on a street corner. They are sold by *Baianas*, women in white lace blouses and skirts, the attire of the sisterhood of the Afro-Bahian religious sect known as *Condomblé*. Those women are usually seated in makeshift stands near a curb selling *acarajé*, along with *abara*, a baked version, and *cocada*, a coconut candy (page 30).

Acarajé is also one of the favorite dishes of *Yansã*, goddess of the waters, storms, and the winds in the *Comdomblé* religion. *Yansã* syncretizes in the Catholic religion with Santa Barbara, and in Cuba with Our Lady of the Lights who dispenses all types of drinks.

Since my first taste of *acarajé* in 1960, I have often prepared them at home for friends. They are always a popular item on my Bahian buffet tables.

2 POUNDS DRY BLACK-EYED PEAS (5 CUPS)	2 GARLIC CLOVES
2 LARGE ONIONS	2 TEASPOONS SALT
½ CUP DRIED SHRIMP	PALM OIL FOR FRYING

Soak the black-eyed peas for 6 hours or overnight in water to cover. Remove the skins by rubbing the peas with your hands to loosen the skins or place them in a towel and lightly press with a rolling pin. Discard the skins.

Soak the dried shrimp in warm water for 10 minutes. Drain and dry the shrimp. Put the beans through a meat grinder or food processor with the onion, shrimp, and garlic, using a small blade until the mixture resembles a purée. Mix well and add the salt. Beat with a wooden spoon or electric mixer until fluffy. Add a little of the shrimp water if necessary.

Heat 4 inches of the oil in a deep fryer or pot. Drop heaping tablespoonfuls of the batter into the hot oil and fry until they float and are golden. Drain on paper towels. Make a slit in one side and insert a teaspoon of the *acarajé sauce* or *vatapa* (page 64). Serve at room temperature.

Acarajé Sauce

Molho de Acarajé
MAKES 3 CUPS

1 CUP DRIED SHRIMP	1 TEASPOON SALT
2 DRIED *MALAGUETA* PEPPERS OR 2	½ CUP PALM OIL
TABLESPOONS HOT PEPPER FLAKES	1 CUP SMALL FRESH SHRIMP, COARSELY
2 GARLIC CLOVES	CHOPPED (ABOUT ½ POUND)
1 MEDIUM ONION, CHOPPED	

Soak the dried shrimp in warm water for 10 minutes. Drain and place it in a
blender with the peppers, garlic, onion, and salt. Blend to a purée.

Heat the oil in a skillet, add the fresh shrimp and cook about 2 minutes, stirring
occasionally. Add the dried shrimp purée, mix well and simmer for about 3
minutes. Cool.

NOTE: This sauce can also be served with *Arroz-de-Hauça* (page 74), *Xinxim de
Galinha* (page 48), and *Vatapa* (page 64).

Rice *and* Sardine Croquettes

Bolinhos de Arroz com Sardinhas
MAKES ABOUT 4 DOZEN

THESE APPETIZERS ARE POPULAR in the Northeast as well as other parts of Brazil and throughout the Portuguese-speaking world. In São Tomé and Príncipe, located in the Guiné Gulf of Africa, manioc is used instead of rice. In Mozambique, chopped shrimp is used instead of sardines, and in Portugal, fish is added to a dough made with flour and eggs, which is then deep fried. The combination of rice and sardines may seem a bit unusual, but they make a delicious appetizer.

4 CUPS COLD COOKED RICE	SALT AND BLACK PEPPER
1 CUP FRESHLY GRATED PARMESAN CHEESE (ABOUT 6 OUNCES)	VEGETABLE OIL FOR FRYING
6 (4½-OUNCE) CANS BONELESS AND SKINLESS SARDINES, DRAINED	COATING:
3 EGGS, LIGHTLY BEATEN	2 EGGS, LIGHTLY BEATEN
	2 CUPS DRY BREAD CRUMBS

In a large pot, mix the rice, cheese, sardines, and eggs until well incorporated. Place the pot over low heat and cook, stirring constantly, until the mixture is thick enough to form a croquette. Add salt and black pepper to taste and mix well.

Cool the mixture and shape into balls the size of walnuts. In a deep skillet, heat the oil 3 inches deep. Dip the balls in the beaten eggs and roll in the crumbs. Fry in the hot oil until golden. Drain on paper towels and serve at room temperature.

NOTE: I occasionally substitute Asiago or cheddar cheese for a sharper flavor.

Shrimp Empanadas

Empadas de Camarão
MAKES ABOUT 24

THESE TASTY APPETIZERS are served in many Brazilian homes, rich and poor. They usually take on the name of the lady of the house, such as *Empadas de Camarão de Maria* (Maria's shrimp empanadas). *Empadas* are served for special occasions, and can also be found in restaurants. I have even sampled them at corner taverns served with drinks. They are easy to prepare with a food processor.

SHRIMP:
JUICE OF 1 LEMON
4 LARGE GARLIC CLOVES, MINCED
1 TEASPOON SALT
¼ TEASPOON BLACK PEPPER
½ POUND SMALL SHRIMP, PEELED AND
  CHOPPED

DOUGH:
2 CUPS FLOUR
1 TEASPOON SALT
1 EGG YOLK
1 CUP (2 STICKS) BUTTER, SOFTENED

FILLING:
2 MEDIUM RIPE TOMATOES, PEELED
  AND QUARTERED
2 MEDIUM ONIONS, QUARTERED
2 GARLIC CLOVES
½ GREEN BELL PEPPER, QUARTERED
¼ CUP FRESH PARSLEY LEAVES
3 TABLESPOONS OLIVE OIL
½ CUP PITTED BLACK OLIVES,
  QUARTERED
1 TABLESPOON TOMATO PASTE
½ TEASPOON TABASCO SAUCE OR
  OTHER HOT SAUCE
1 TEASPOON FLOUR
1 EGG YOLK, LIGHTLY BEATEN

FOR THE SHRIMP: Mix the lemon juice, garlic, salt, and pepper together in a 1-quart bowl. Add the shrimp and set aside while you prepare the pastry.

FOR THE DOUGH: Mix the flour and salt in a medium-size bowl. Add 3 tablespoons water, the egg yolk, and butter. Stir until a soft dough forms. Knead the dough for 5 minutes. Set aside for 1 hour.

FOR THE FILLING: In a food processor, or by hand, mince the tomatoes, onions, garlic, green peppers, and parsley. Heat the olive oil in a 10-inch skillet and add the vegetable mixture. Stir well and add the shrimp mixture and the olives. Simmer for 10 minutes. In a small bowl mix ¼ cup water, the tomato paste, and Tabasco sauce, and add it to the shrimp mixture. Add the flour to thicken the filling. Remove from the heat and cool, about 20 minutes.

Preheat the oven to 450°F. Roll out the dough on a floured surface to about ⅛ inch thick. Using a 4-inch round cutter, cut rounds and line 24 muffin tins with the circles of dough. Fill each with about 2 tablespoons of the shrimp mixture. Top with another round of pastry; pinch the sides together and brush with the beaten egg yolk. Bake for 20 minutes. Cool on racks for 5 minutes and serve at room temperature.

Beef Croquettes

Bolinhos de Carne
MAKES 20 TO 30

EVEN IN THE YEARS WHEN MOST HOUSEHOLDS HAD COOKS, it took 3 hours to prepare beef croquettes and they were reserved for parties and festive occasions. Today, many women work and help is much more expensive and harder to find. Because these croquettes are time consuming to prepare, many housewives purchase them already prepared at delis and supermarkets. This particular recipe uses preground beef and, because it doesn't call for a stuffing, is less time-consuming. The end result is delicious.

⅓ CUP VEGETABLE OIL	1 MEDIUM POTATO, PEELED, COOKED,
1½ POUNDS GROUND BEEF	AND MASHED
¼ CUP GRATED ONION	¼ CUP FLOUR
2 GARLIC CLOVES, MINCED	
1 LARGE TOMATO, PEELED, SEEDED,	COATING:
AND MINCED	2 EGGS, LIGHTLY BEATEN
SALT AND BLACK PEPPER	2 TEASPOONS MILK
2 TABLESPOONS CHOPPED FRESH PARSLEY	2 CUPS FLOUR
	VEGETABLE OIL FOR FRYING

In a large non-stick skillet, heat the oil and sauté the ground beef, onion, garlic, and tomato. Cook, stirring until the beef is cooked through and the onions are translucent. Mix in salt and pepper to taste and the parsley. Lower the heat and add the mashed potato and flour, stirring constantly until the dough comes away from the sides of the pan. Remove from the heat and cool.

Beat the eggs with the milk in a shallow bowl. Place the flour in another shallow bowl. Heat the vegetable oil about 3 to 4 inches deep in a deep skillet. Using 2 tablespoons, form the dough into egg shapes. Roll the croquettes first in the egg mixture and then in the flour. Fry in the oil until golden. Serve at room temperature.

NOTE: These croquettes can also be made with leftover roast beef. In that case, grind the meat in a meat grinder then mix with the onions, garlic, tomatoes, salt, and black pepper and proceed with the recipe. Ground chicken also works well.

Bahian Egg Ragout

Moqueca de Ovos
3 TO 5 SERVINGS

MOQUECA OR *MUKEKA*, a Kimbundo word from Angola, originally referred to a meat or fish stew, ragout, or fricassee. As this recipe exemplifies, after it arrived in Brazil, *mukeka* came to encompass a variety of ragout-type dishes, including this meatless one. Serve for breakfast or lunch.

3 TABLESPOONS PALM OIL	½ CUP CHOPPED FRESH PARSLEY
1 LARGE ONION, MINCED	¼ CUP CHOPPED FRESH CILANTRO
2 LARGE TOMATOES, PEELED, SEEDED	5 EGG YOLKS, UNBROKEN
AND CHOPPED	SALT AND BLACK PEPPER

Heat the palm oil in a large skillet and sauté the onion. Cook until translucent and add the tomatoes, parsley, and cilantro. When the sauce begins to boil, carefully add the egg yolks placed strategically around the pan. Season each yolk with salt and black pepper, lower the heat and cook until the egg yolks are cooked to your liking, hard or soft.

Place a spoonful of onions and a yolk on each plate and serve with sausage or bacon.

Bahian-Style Chicken

Xinxim de Galinha

4 TO 6 SERVINGS

XINXIM DE GALINHA is another Afro-Brazilian dish of Nigerian origin. It is popular in the North and Northeast, but nowhere is it prepared like it is in Bahia. I first tasted *xinxim* in 1961 in the home of a dear friend, Norma Sampaio. Later that year I attended a *Condomblé* ceremony at the cult house of the famous priestess Olga de Alaqueta and had another opportunity to taste this dish, and to observe the preparation. The dish was prepared in honor of *Oxum*, a Yoruba water goddess.

This recipe is very similar to the one I tasted at Olga's, but instead of a whole chicken, I use a combination of breasts and thighs.

---

4 CHICKEN BREASTS AND 4 CHICKEN
  THIGHS (3 POUNDS TOTAL)
1 TEASPOON SALT
6 GARLIC CLOVES, CHOPPED
JUICE OF 1 LEMON

1 MEDIUM ONION, CHOPPED
1 CUP DRIED SHRIMP
1 CUP UNSALTED ROASTED PEANUTS
  (6 OUNCES)
1 CUP PALM OIL

Rinse the chicken pieces and dry well. Mix the salt with 3 of the garlic cloves and grind to a paste in a mortar and pestle. Add the lemon juice, mix well and rub into the chicken. In a meat grinder or food processor purée the onion, 3 remaining garlic cloves, dried shrimp, and roasted peanuts.

Heat the palm oil in a large skillet. Add the puréed ingredients and simmer for 5 minutes, stirring occasionally. Add the chicken and ¼ cup water. Mix well and cook for 30 minutes, uncovered. Stir occasionally and add water if the sauce begins to dry out. Serve with Toasted Manioc Meal with Palm Oil (page 40) and rice.

Beef-Stuffed Manioc Balls

Bolinho de Macaxeira Recheado
MAKES ABOUT 24

MANIOC WAS A STAPLE in the early days of colonization and continues to be popular in this northeast territory today. *Macaxeira* is an indigenous name for manioc.

DOUGH:	FILLING:
2 POUNDS MANIOC ROOT	½ POUND GROUND BEEF
1 TEASPOON SALT	¼ CUP MINCED ONION
2 EGGS	3 GARLIC CLOVES, MINCED
1 TABLESPOON BUTTER	¼ CUP CHOPPED FRESH PARSLEY
1 CUP FLOUR	1 TABLESPOON DRIED ROSEMARY
½ CUP GRATED PARMESAN CHEESE	1 TEASPOON BLACK PEPPER
(3½ OUNCES)	CORN OR CANOLA OIL FOR FRYING

FOR THE DOUGH: Peel the manioc root, cut into cubes, removing the core. Bring to a boil in water to cover with 1 teaspoon salt, cook until tender. Drain the manioc and mash with a fork or put through a ricer. Add the eggs, one at a time, the butter, flour, and cheese mixing well after each addition.

FOR THE FILLING: Heat a nonstick skillet and saute the beef with the onions, garlic, parsley, rosemary, and pepper. Cook, stirring, until the beef is cooked through and the onions are translucent.

With a tablespoon, scoop up balls of dough the size of an egg. Make an indentation with your thumb and insert 1 teaspoon of the filling. Pinch the dough closed over the filling. Heat the oil 3 inches deep to 350°F. Fry the balls in the oil until golden.

NOTE: Traditionally, this recipe called for a cheese made from goat's milk, which was prepared in each household. Today most cooks use Parmesan cheese because it is readily available and has a similar flavor. These balls can also be prepared without the meat filling. In that case, increase the eggs to 3 and the Parmesan cheese to 1 cup. Add 1 teaspoon baking powder to the flour mixture.

Ground Beef Pie

Frigideira de Carne

6 TO 8 SERVINGS

THIS BEEF PIE IS WONDERFUL for a Sunday brunch, but it is also found on many a Bahian buffet table at festive occasions. For brunch or a light meal, serve with a green salad.

2 POUNDS STEW BEEF	6 EGGS, SEPARATED
2 TABLESPOONS WHITE VINEGAR	1 TABLESPOON VEGETABLE OIL
2 GARLIC CLOVES, MINCED	
1 TEASPOON SALT	GARNISH:
1 TABLESPOON LARD OR SHORTENING	1 TOMATO, SEEDED AND CUT INTO
2 SLICES SMOKED BACON, MINCED	6 SLICES
(OPTIONAL)	1 GREEN BELL PEPPER, SEEDED AND
1 LARGE ONION, MINCED	CUT WIDTHWISE INTO 6 SLICES
2 CHAYOTES, PEELED AND CHOPPED	1 WHITE ONION, CUT INTO 6 SLICES
4 MEDIUM TOMATOES, PEELED AND	
CHOPPED	

Trim the fat from the beef and cut into in 1-inch cubes. Sprinkle the vinegar over the meat. Pound the garlic and salt to a paste in a mortar and pestle. Mix the paste with the beef and set aside in the refrigerator for 30 minutes.

Preheat the oven to 375°F.

Melt the lard in a large skillet and fry the bacon. Add the onion and cook until lightly golden. Add the beef, chayote, and tomato. Cover and cook over medium heat until the beef is lightly browned. Remove from the heat and cool. Put the meat mixture through the coarse disk of a meat grinder or process in a food processor. Set aside.

Beat the egg whites until stiff. Beat the yolks until foamy and fold into the whites. Fold ¼ cup egg into the meat mixture, and cover with the remaining eggs. Bake until the top is golden brown. Remove from the oven and decorate with tomato, green pepper, and onion rings. Return to the oven for 5 minutes. Serve warm.

NOTE: Remove the centers from the tomato, pepper, and onion slices so that only the outer ring remains. Arrange the tomato, pepper, and onion slices in concentric circles on top of the pie. Turkey bacon can be substituted for regular bacon.

Bahian Stew

Cozido

18 TO 20 SERVINGS

THIS IS THE BRAZILIAN VERSION OF *COZIDO À PORTUGUESA* (Portuguese-style stew). The amount of ingredients depends on the number of guests. It is perfect for a large dinner party of anywhere between ten and twenty. My last memorable *cozido* was enjoyed at the home of my friends Silvio and Lia Robatto in Salvador, Bahia in 2001. It is best to begin preparing the stew a day in advance so that the chicken and meats can marinate overnight. Serve the stew with Pepper and Lemon Sauce (page 39).

MARINADE:
4 GARLIC CLOVES
2 TEASPOONS SALT
½ CUP PARSLEY LEAVES
¼ CUP CILANTRO LEAVES
3 ONIONS, CHOPPED
1 CUP WHITE VINEGAR
3 BAY LEAVES, CRUSHED
1 TEASPOON WHOLE CORIANDER
 SEEDS

INGREDIENTS:
4 POUNDS CHICKEN THIGHS
1 (3-POUND) BEEF RUMP ROAST
3 POUNDS LEAN CHUCK ROAST
4 TABLESPOONS LARD, SHORTENING
 OR VEGETABLE OIL

4 LARGE TOMATOES, CHOPPED
3 MEDIUM ONIONS
1 HAM BONE
3 POUNDS SMOKED PORK SAUSAGES
2 POUNDS PORK LOIN
3 POUNDS FRESH PORK SAUSAGES
3 POUNDS MANIOC ROOT, PEELED
6 SWEET POTATOES, PEELED
9 MEDIUM BOILING POTATOES, PEELED
1 LARGE HEAD CABBAGE, QUARTERED
6 MEDIUM TURNIPS, PEELED
2 POUNDS GREEN BEANS, TRIMMED
3 POUNDS BUTTERNUT SQUASH,
 PEELED
2 POUNDS FRESH OKRA, TRIMMED
10 PLANTAINS, PEELED AND HALVED
MANIOC FLOUR

Crush the garlic and salt in a mortar and pestle and place in a bowl with the parsley, cilantro, onions, vinegar, and bay leaves. Crush the coriander seeds with the mortar and pestle and add them to the mixture. Place the chicken thighs in one large bowl and the beef and chuck roast in another. Divide the marinade between the two bowls and rub into the meats. Marinate the meats in the refrigerator for at least 6 hours or overnight.

The following morning remove the chicken from the marinade. Melt 2 table-spoons of the shortening in a large saucepan and brown the chicken on all sides. In another large saucepan, heat the remaining 2 tablespoons shortening and brown the meats. Add 2 cups water to each pot, cover and simmer for 1 hour.

Remove the meats and liquid and combine in a deep 6-quart pot. Add the tomato, onion, ham bone, and water to cover, and simmer until the meats are tender. Add the smoked pork sausages, pork loin, fresh pork sausages, manioc root, whole sweet potatoes, whole white potatoes, cabbage, turnips, and green beans. Add enough water to cover the vegetables and season to taste. Cover the pot and simmer over low heat. Remove the vegetables from the pot as they are cooked and keep them warm. When all vegetables have been removed from the pot, add the squash, okra, and the plantains and continue simmering.

To serve, place the chicken pieces in the center of a large platter. Slice the beef and arrange it around the chicken. Arrange half of the vegetables around the meats. Slice the pork loin and place in the center of another platter. Arrange the remaining vegetables around the pork loin. Cut the sausages into 1-inch pieces and place around the vegetables.

Place 2 cups broth in a small pot. Mash enough sweet potatoes to make ¼ cup, mix it into the broth, and pour the broth over the vegetables and meats. With the remaining broth make a manioc purée (page 66). Use 1 cup manioc flour for each 2 cups of broth. Serve the purée in a separate dish.

Bahian Bean Stew

Feijoada Baiana
20 SERVINGS

FEIJOADA, THE NATIONAL DISH OF BRAZIL was created in the slave quarters of Bahia and is enjoyed throughout the country. In the northeast, *feijoada* is made with brown beans called *mulatinhos*, and in the south black beans are the norm. It is very probable that the Portuguese took this dish from Brazil to other parts of the Portuguese-speaking world. In Portugal's northwestern province, Trás-os-Montes, there is a version of *feijoada* made with kidney beans. There is a variation of *feijoada* in Mozambique, East Timor, and Goa and a *cachupa* in Cape Verde, which calls for corn, fava beans, hominy, and Great Northern beans.

In the northeast, *feijoada* is popular for lunch on Ash Wednesday when the first smoked meat of the year is eaten. It is also traditionally served for lunch on Saturdays, special occasions, and large parties.

Begin preparation at least one day in advance. This gives you time to prepare all the accompanying dishes and also allows for the flavors to meld. Even though this can be time-consuming, the end result is well worth the effort.

4 POUNDS DRY BROWN OR BLACK BEANS (8 CUPS)	2 POUNDS FRESH PORK SAUSAGES
2 POUNDS BRAZILIAN DRIED BEEF	2 POUNDS SMOKED PORTUGUESE SAUSAGES
2 POUNDS *PAIO* OR CANADIAN BACON	1 TABLESPOON SHORTENING OR VEGETABLE OIL
1 (6-POUND) PORK LOIN ROAST	4 GARLIC CLOVES, MINCED
3 LARGE ONIONS, 1 SLICED AND 2 CHOPPED	1 LARGE TOMATO, CHOPPED
SALT AND BLACK PEPPER	1 TABLESPOON CHOPPED FRESH PARSLEY
GARLIC POWDER	2 TABLESPOONS CRUSHED RED PEPPER
2 CUPS WHITE WINE	
2 BAY LEAVES	

The day before serving, pick over the beans. Rinse and soak them in cold water for 6 hours or overnight. Soak the dried beef and *paio* separately in cold water overnight or for 6 hours in the refrigerator. Wash the pork loin and pat dry. Arrange half the onion slices on the bottom of a glass baking dish large enough to hold the pork loin. Set the pork on top of the onions and sprinkle with salt, pepper, and garlic powder. Pour the wine over the pork, add the bay leaf, and lay the remaining onion slices over the pork. Marinate in the refrigerator, covered, for 6 hours or overnight.

The following day, drain the beans, place in a pot, cover with fresh cold water and cook, covered, for about 2½ hours, adding water as needed to keep the beans covered. As soon as the beans begin to cook, cut the dried beef into 1½-inch cubes and add to the beans.

Preheat the oven to 350°F. Prick the fresh sausages and set aside. Blanche the Canadian bacon and smoked sausages and set aside. Remove the pork loin from the refrigerator and roast, covered, in the oven for 1 hour. Remove the cover and continue roasting until the pork browns a bit, about ½ hour, basting occasionally.

Add all the meats except the pork loin to the beans during the last hour of cooking and simmer until the meats are tender. Season with salt to taste.

About ½ hour before serving, melt the shortening in a large skillet and gently sauté the chopped onions, garlic, tomato, parsley, and red pepper. Add about 1 cup of the beans and mash with a wooden spoon. Pour about 2 cups of the bean cooking liquid over the mixture and simmer until the mixture thickens. Add the mixture to the pot of beans. Simmer until thoroughly blended, about 10 minutes. Taste and correct the seasonings.

To serve: Remove the meats from the beans and pour the beans into a large chafing dish or soup tureen. Place the pork loin in the center of a large platter and thinly slice. Slice the sausages into ½-inch pieces and place on one side of the pork loin. Slice the Canadian bacon and place on the platter with the dried beef. Serve with orange wedges, Toasted Manioc Meal (page 40), white rice, Minas-Style Collard Greens (page 113), Pepper and Lemon Sauce (page 89), and a Caipirinha (page 85).

Minced Dried Beef

Paçoca de Carne Pernambucana

4 SERVINGS

IN THE BACKLANDS OF THE NORTHEAST, *paçoca* (dried beef) was traditionally ground with a mortar and pestle until thoroughly pulverized before it
was eaten. Today, this dish has become popular in the larger cities because
homemakers have the use of a food processor to facilitate the chore. *Paçoca*
is usually served with Marie-Isabel Rice (page 77).

2 POUNDS DRIED BRAZILIAN BEEF	¼ CUP CHOPPED FRESH PARSLEY
½ CUP CLARIFIED BUTTER	¼ CUP CHOPPED GREEN ONIONS
1 MEDIUM ONION, CHOPPED	
½ CUP MANIOC FLOUR	

Soak the dried beef for 6 hours or overnight covered with water. The following
day, trim the beef of all fat and cut into 1-inch cubes. Place the beef cubes in a
pot, cover with water and boil for 10 minutes. Remove and place in a large
frying pan. Add the butter and onion and cook until the onion is golden
brown. Stir in the manioc flour. Remove from the heat and allow the mixture
to cool. Transfer the mixture to a food processor, in small quantities, and
blend until the mixture resembles coarse meal. Place in a serving dish and garnish with the parsley and spring onions.

Braised Goat

Cabrito a pé de Serra

4 SERVINGS

IN THE BACKLANDS OF THE STATE OF CEARÁ, this dish is prepared in many well known restaurants. The goat leg is marinated overnight to impregnate it with the seasonings.

1 (3-POUND) LEG OF GOAT (UPPER THIGH)	1 BAY LEAF
2 CUPS RED WINE	½ CUP CHOPPED FRESH PARSLEY
1 MEDIUM CARROT, PEELED AND MINCED	½ CUP CHOPPED GREEN ONIONS
1 MEDIUM ONION, MINCED	1 TEASPOON SALT
½ CUP MINCED FRESH CILANTRO	BLACK PEPPER
	¼ CUP OLIVE OIL
	2 CUPS HOT WATER OR BEEF BROTH

Place the goat in a large bowl and add the wine, carrots, onions, cilantro, bay leaf, parsley, green onions, salt, and pepper to taste. Cover with plastic wrap and place in the refrigerator for 48 hours, turning at least 4 times.

In a large skillet heat the olive oil over medium heat. Remove the goat from the marinade and place in the hot oil. Turn occasionally to ensure browning on all sides. Add the reserved marinade and 2 cups of hot water or beef broth a little at a time and simmer until the goat meat is cooked, about 2 hours. Let the liquid evaporate so that the goat browns in the fat left in the pan and is golden and crusty on all sides.

Serve with broccoli rice (page 76) and steamed or boiled potatoes.

Pernambuco-Style Fish Steaks

Peixada Pernambucana

6 SERVINGS

THIS RECIPE FOR FISH STEAKS prepared with fresh vegetables, is a popular dish in Pernambuco. It is a perfect dish for a noon meal on a hot day.

FISH:	6 MEDIUM CARROTS, JULIENNED
6 FISH STEAKS (GROUPER, HALIBUT,	3 CHAYOTES, JULIENNED
OR SALMON)	1 TEASPOON SALT
JUICE OF 2 LEMONS	
2 GARLIC CLOVES, CRUSHED	VINAIGRETTE:
1 TEASPOON SALT	3 GARLIC CLOVES, MINCED
¼ TEASPOON BLACK PEPPER	1 TEASPOON SALT
1 BUNCH CILANTRO, STEMMED	2 TABLESPOONS WHITE VINEGAR
1 POUND FRENCH-STYLE GREEN	6 TABLESPOONS OLIVE OIL
BEANS (HARICOTS VERTS)	2 DROPS HOT PEPPER SAUCE

FOR THE FISH: Place the fish steaks in a non-reactive bowl. Mix the lemon juice, garlic, salt, and pepper together, and pour over the fish. Let marinate for 1 hour in the refrigerator. Place the fish steaks in a single layer in 1 large or 2 medium-size skillets. Sprinkle with the cilantro leaves and add water to barely cover. Bring to a low boil and simmer for 10 minutes.

Meanwhile, tie the vegetables in separate bundles and place in a pot of boiling water with the salt. Return to a boil. After 15 minutes remove the chayotes; after 20 minutes remove the green beans; and after 30 minutes remove the carrots.

FOR THE VINAIGRETTE: Purée the garlic and salt in a mortar and pestle. Add the vinegar to the purée and mix well. Whisk in the olive oil in a slow stream, then season with the hot pepper sauce. Stir to incorporate. Set aside.

Arrange 1 fish steak on each plate. Surround the fish with vegetables in a decorative manner. Pour the vinaigrette over the fish and vegetables and serve immediately.

NOTE: This dish is traditionally served with a Portuguese *vinho verde*.

Ceará-Style Fish *in* Broth

Peixada

8 SERVINGS

THIS RECIPE IS SIMILAR TO A *MOQUECA* or fish stew (page 60) which is very popular in the state of Bahia. *Peixada* calls for olive oil instead of the palm oil so common in many Afro-Brazilian dishes. It is served with a very tasty seasoned broth.

STOCK:	FISH:
3 FISH HEADS (ABOUT 2 POUNDS)	4 POUNDS GROUPER FILLETS
1 CUP CILANTRO LEAVES	¼ CUP LEMON JUICE
4 GREEN ONIONS, CHOPPED	2 TEASPOONS SALT
3 TOMATOES, PEELED AND CHOPPED	1 TEASPOON BLACK PEPPER
1 TEASPOON SALT	¼ CUP PLUS 2 TABLESPOONS OLIVE OIL
1 TEASPOON WHOLE BLACK	2 LARGE ONIONS, SLICED
PEPPERCORNS	1 CUP CHOPPED FRESH CILANTRO
	SAUCE:
	6 EGG YOLKS
	2 CUPS FISH BOUILLON

FOR THE STOCK: Place the fish heads in a large pot with 2 quarts water, the cilantro, green onions, tomatoes, salt, and peppercorns. Cook over medium heat until the meat falls off the bones, about 1 hour. Remove the bones.

FOR THE FISH: Season the fillets with lemon juice, salt, and pepper. Heat 2 tablespoons of the olive oil in a large skillet. Sauté the fish in the skillet and cover with the onion slices. Sprinkle with the cilantro and pour the remaining olive oil over fish. Cover the pan and cook over medium heat until the fish is tender.

FOR THE SAUCE: Stir the yolks into the fish stock and heat over very low heat. Stir until the stock thickens, but do not boil. Set aside.

TO SERVE: Place the fish on a warm platter. Pour the sauce over the fish or serve on the side. White rice is a traditional accompaniment.

Bahian Fish Ragout

Moqueca de Peixe

4 TO 6 SERVINGS

THE WORD *MOQUECA* probably comes from the Tupi-Guarani word *poke-ka*, although the dish itself is of African origin. It was originally a ragout of fish cooked in palm oil with peppers, then wrapped in banana leaves, and roasted in hot coals. Today this classic dish is usually cooked, without the banana leaves, on top of the stove.

FISH:	1 TEASPOON SALT
2½ POUNDS FISH FILLETS	JUICE OF 1 LEMON
4 GARLIC CLOVES	
1 SMALL TOMATO, CHOPPED	SAUCE:
1 SMALL ONION, CHOPPED	1 LARGE ONION, THINLY SLICED
1 SPRIG CILANTRO, CHOPPED	2 MEDIUM TOMATOES, THINLY SLICED
1 TEASPOON WHOLE BLACK	2 GREEN BELL PEPPERS, THINLY
PEPPERCORNS	SLICED
1 TEASPOON CRUSHED RED PEPPER	1 CUP UNSWEETENED COCONUT MILK
FLAKES	½ CUP PALM OR OLIVE OIL

FOR THE FISH: Dry the fish and cut into serving pieces. In a food processor, purée the garlic, tomato, onion, cilantro, peppercorns, red pepper flakes, and salt. Add the lemon juice and mix well. Pour the mixture over the fish and marinate in the refrigerator for 2 hours, turning occasionally.

FOR THE SAUCE: Place the fish fillets in a large skillet. Top with the onion, tomato, and green pepper slices, and pour the coconut milk and oil over vegetables. Cover and cook over medium heat, for about 6 minutes, until the fish flakes easily.

Bahian-Style Shrimp *and* Okra

Caruru da Bahia

6 TO 8 SERVINGS

IN THE CITY OF SALVADOR, Bahia, this okra-based dish figures importantly in Afro-Brazilian religious ceremonies where it is known as *amalá*. It is preferred by *Xango*, the majestic Yoruba African god of fire and lightening. *Caruru* is also the main dish served during the September festivities in honor of Cosme and Damien, the twin saints of Bahian Afro-Catholic tradition. This old and unique festival, known as "*caruru* of Cosme and Damien" is observed by families with twins. The head of the household invites friends to enjoy a *caruru* in honor of the family's twins and to venerate Cosme and Damien.

1 POUND DRIED SHRIMP	6 LARGE GARLIC CLOVES
1 POUND FISH FILLETS (COD,	½ CUP PALM OIL
GROUPER, OR ANY WHITE FISH)	2 POUNDS OKRA, TRIMMED AND
3 TABLESPOONS LEMON JUICE	THINLY SLICED
1 TEASPOON SALT	1 POUND FRESH SHRIMP IN SHELLS,
½ CUP RAW PEANUTS (3 OUNCES)	BOILED IN SALTED WATER, THEN
2 MEDIUM ONIONS, CHOPPED	PEELED

Preheat the oven to 375°F.

Soak the dried shrimp in warm water to cover for 20 minutes.

Rinse the fish in cold water and pat dry with paper towels. Place the fish in a shallow dish and marinate in the lemon juice and salt for 30 minutes.

Spread the peanuts on a baking sheet and toast in the oven until lightly brown, shaking occasionally, about 10 minutes.

Using the smallest disk of a meat grinder or food processor, grind the dried shrimp, peanuts, onions, and garlic to a purée. Heat the palm oil in a large, deep skillet. Add the peanut mixture and sauté over medium heat, stirring constantly, for 5 minutes. Lower the heat, add the okra and season with salt. Cook for about 20 minutes, stirring occasionally, adding more water if the mixture starts to dry out. Add the fresh shrimp and the fish. Simmer for 10 minutes. Serve with white rice.

Maranhão-Style Shrimp *and* Okra

Caruru de Maranhão

8 SERVINGS

THIS VERSION OF *CARURU* from the state of Maranhão calls for olive oil and manioc flour instead of the palm oil and ground roasted peanuts used for Afro-Bahian dishes in religious ceremonies in Bahia.

2 CUPS DRIED SHRIMP	2 SMALL ONIONS, MINCED
2 POUNDS OKRA, CUT INTO 1-INCH	4 GARLIC CLOVES, MINCED
SLICES	1 POUND FRESH SHRIMP, PEELED
¼ CUP MANIOC FLOUR	AND DEVEINED
¼ CUP OLIVE OIL	1 TEASPOON SALT

Soak the dried shrimp in warm water for 30 minutes to remove excess salt. Process half the dried shrimp in a food processor or put through a meat grinder to purée. Set aside.

In a large pot, bring 4 cups water to a boil over high heat, add the okra and cook for about 5 minutes. Remove from the heat, drain, reserving the water, and set aside.

In the same pot, bring the reserved water to a boil. Slowly pour the manioc flour into the water, stirring constantly so no lumps form. Set aside.

In a large skillet heat the olive oil over medium heat. Add the onions and garlic and cook until the onions are lightly browned. Add the whole dried shrimp and the fresh shrimp and cook for 3 minutes, stirring continually. Remove from the heat.

Return the manioc mixture to the heat and cook, stirring, until the mixture is the consistency of oatmeal. Add to the shrimp mixture. Add the okra and puréed dried shrimp. Mix well, season with salt and cook until heated through. Serve with white rice.

NOTE: By boiling the okra separately you can eliminate the so-called slime. Just skim off any foam that collects on the surface of the water. If you like a dish with a little zing, sprinkle the dish with a little hot sauce or ground red pepper.

Shrimp Torte

Torta de Camarões

6 SERVINGS

THIS IS ANOTHER RECIPE USING THE TASTY SHRIMP that are so plentiful in the waters off the coast of Maranhão. This torte is easy to prepare and with the exception of shrimp, uses ingredients that one usually has on hand.

2 TABLESPOONS OLIVE OIL	½ CUP CHOPPED GREEN ONIONS
1 GREEN BELL PEPPER, SEEDED AND CHOPPED	1 POUND SHRIMP, SHELLED AND DEVEINED
2 TOMATOES, PEELED AND CHOPPED	5 EGGS, SEPARATED
½ CUP CHOPPED FRESH PARSLEY	

Heat the oven to 350°F and grease a 10-inch pie pan.

Heat the olive oil in a large skillet and add the green pepper, tomato, parsley, and green onion. Cook over medium heat stirring, until the vegetables are soft. Add the shrimp and cook until pink, stirring continually. Remove from the heat and set aside.

Place the egg whites in a medium-size bowl and beat until stiff peaks form. In a separate bowl, beat the egg yolks until foamy. Fold the yolks into the whites, then fold in the shrimp mixture. Turn the mixture into the prepared pan.

Bake until lightly browned, about 20 minutes. Remove and place on a rack to cool for 5 minutes. Remove from the pan and place on a serving platter.

Bahian Shrimp *and* Bread Pudding

Vatapá
10 SERVINGS

DURING COLONIAL TIMES *vatapá* was one of the best-loved Afro-Brazilian dishes to grace the tables of both masters and slaves. Today, *vatapá* retains its popularity in Bahia, the Afro-Brazilian city where it is served on many ceremonial occasions and appears on the menu of most restaurants featuring Bahian cuisine. To quote Manuel Querino, a Bahian scholar: "The palate is more appreciative than the senses. Music may go in one ear and out the other. The vision of a beautiful picture soon disappears from a short memory. But the remembrance of a good *Vatapá* is eternal." *Vatapá* is the preferred food of Ogum, the Yoruba god of War and Iron (his Catholic counterpart is St. Anthony). He likes it prepared in the traditional way with cashews, peanuts, dried shrimp, coconut milk, bread, onions, and palm oil.

I had the pleasure of eating *vatapá* several times during Afro-Brazilian religious rites in Salvador, such as the Condomblé ceremonies led by Olga de Alaketu, one of Bahia's famous sect priestesses. The late Waldeloir Rego, a good friend and leading authority on Candomblé, believed that what follows is the most authentic of *vatapá* recipes.

Remember, as Dorival Caymmi, the great Bahian vocalist, advises in his classic folk song *Vatapá*, *"Não parar de mexê-o/Que é para não embolar,"* which means "Don't stop stirring/So it doesn't get lumpy!"

FISH:	PUDDING:
JUICE OF 1 LEMON	1 CUP RAW CASHEWS (5½ OUNCES)
2 GARLIC CLOVES, CRUSHED	1 CUP PEANUTS (5½ OUNCES)
1 TEASPOON SALT	½ POUND DRIED SHRIMP
¼ TEASPOON BLACK PEPPER	2 LARGE ONIONS, COARSELY CHOPPED
1 POUND GROUPER OR OTHER WHITE	4 LARGE GARLIC CLOVES
FISH FILLETS	1 LARGE LOAF WHITE BREAD, UNCUT
	(1½ POUNDS)
	1 POUND FRESH SHRIMP, UNPEELED
	¾ CUP PALM OIL
	1 (13½-OUNCE) CAN UNSWEETENED
	COCONUT MILK

FOR THE FISH: Mix together all the marinade ingredients and pour over the fish fillets. Refrigerate for 2 hours.

FOR THE PUDDING: Preheat the oven to 375°F. Place the cashews and peanuts on a baking sheet and toast for about 10 minutes, shaking occasionally, until they are lightly golden.

Soak the dried shrimp in hot water to cover for 10 minutes and drain. Using a meat grinder or food processor, grind the shrimp and set aside. Grind or process the onions and garlic and place in a large bowl. Remove the crust from the bread and break into large pieces. Soak in cold water for 5 minutes. Squeeze the water from the bread and put through the grinder. Set aside. Grind the cashews and the peanuts and add to the bowl with the shrimp mixture.

Place the fresh shrimp, fish, and marinade in a pot with water to cover. Bring to a boil and cook until the shrimp turn pink. Remove the shrimp and fish from the pot and reserve the liquid. Peel the shrimp, flake the fish and set aside. Heat the palm oil in a 10-quart pot. Add the nut mixture. Using a wooden spoon, stir the mixture continuously for 5 minutes. Add the bread and mix well. Pour in half the coconut milk and 1 cup of the reserved liquid, stir well. Continue stirring for 15 to 20 minutes or until the mixture thickens. Add the rest of the coconut milk, the fish, and the shrimp. Cook for another 15 minutes, stirring occasionally. The finished dish should be a thick, orange purée that can be eaten with a fork.

Serve at room temperature.

Shrimp *with* Manioc Purée

Bobó de Camarão

6 TO 8 SERVINGS

THERE ARE VARIOUS WAYS to prepare a *bobó*, which derives from a West African word for a mixture of ingredients. The dish can be prepared with bread fruit, beans, or manioc. When it is combined with an ingredient like shrimp, that gives it a characteristic flavor, it takes on that ingredient's name. In Angola there is an identical dish called *ipété*. Originally this dish was served simply with white rice. Today, many Bahians serve *bobó* as a side dish with grilled fish, chicken, or shrimp, with or without palm oil

---

4 POUNDS MEDIUM-SIZE SHRIMP, PEELED AND DEVEINED, SHELLS RESERVED
1 TEASPOON SALT
½ TEASPOON BLACK PEPPER
JUICE OF 2 LEMONS
3 LARGE ONIONS, 1 ROUGHLY CHOPPED AND 2 MINCED
1 BAY LEAF
1 BUNCH CILANTRO
¼ CUP CHOPPED FRESH PARSLEY
2 POUNDS MANIOC ROOT, PEELED AND GRATED

2 (14-OUNCE) CANS COCONUT MILK
¼ CUP PALM OIL
4 GARLIC CLOVES, MASHED TO A PURÉE
1 POUND TOMATOES, PEELED, SEEDED, AND MINCED
1 LARGE GREEN BELL PEPPER, PEELED, SEEDED, AND MINCED
1 CUP CHOPPED BRAZIL NUTS (6 OUNCES)

Season the shrimp with the salt, pepper, and lemon juice. Place the shrimp shells in a large pot. Add the roughly chopped onion, bay leaf, 1 sprig of cilantro, and half the parsley. Cover with water and bring to a boil. Reduce the heat and simmer until the liquid is reduced by half. Drain the liquid and set aside.

Place the grated manioc in a pot with 1 cup of the reserved shrimp liquid and 1 can of coconut milk. Cook covered, over medium heat, until the manioc becomes a purée. Set aside. The purée will retain a little liquid and as it sits, more liquid will form.

Heat 2 tablespoons of the palm oil in a large skillet. Add the shrimp and sauté, stirring continually, until cooked. Remove from the pan and keep warm. Add the minced onion and the garlic to the pan and cook until the onion is golden. Add the tomatoes and green pepper and cook for 3 minutes. Add the manioc with its liquid and cook over low heat until the tomatoes and peppers are soft. Add the remaining can of coconut milk and the rest of the shrimp liquid to the vegetables and cook another 10 minutes. Add the Brazil nuts, the remaining cilantro and parsley, the shrimp, and remaining 2 tablespoons of palm oil. Simmer for 3 minutes.

Serve with white rice.

NOTE: Some cooks add dried shrimp to the dish. Soak 1 cup dried shrimp in warm water for 10 minutes. Drain and grind or process to a purée. Add to the pan with the onion and garlic and continue with the rest of the recipe.

Baked Crab Omelet

Frigideira de Siri

6 SERVINGS

AFRICAN SLAVES ALTERED A NUMBER of traditional Portuguese dishes by using their own spices, herbs, and other ingredients. To dishes like *frigideira* they added coconut milk and cashews, and substituted palm oil for olive oil.

In Brazil, the name *frigideira* or *fritada* is given to any baked dish with chopped ingredients covered with beaten eggs. The most popular of these dishes are made with shrimp, codfish, crabmeat, fish, or *linguiça* (sausage). *Frigideiras* are common throughout the Portuguese-speaking world: Shrimp Pudding in Mozambique, Oyster Pie in Goa, and Black Swordfish Pudding in Madeira.

1 (14-OUNCE) CAN UNSWEETENED COCONUT MILK	1 TABLESPOON CHOPPED FRESH PARSLEY
2 (1-INCH) SLICES OF STALE FRENCH BREAD	6 EGGS, SEPARATED
1 POUND CRABMEAT	SALT AND BLACK PEPPER
2 MEDIUM ONIONS, CHOPPED	
1 TEASPOON SALT	GARNISH:
¼ TEASPOON BLACK PEPPER	1 GREEN BELL PEPPER, SEEDED AND SLICED WIDTHWISE INTO 6 SLICES
2 LARGE GARLIC CLOVES, MINCED	1 TOMATO, CUT INTO 6 SLICES
3 TABLESPOONS LEMON JUICE	6 GREEN PIMENTO-STUFFED OLIVES, SLICED
2 TABLESPOONS OLIVE OIL	
2 CHAYOTES, PEELED AND CHOPPED	
2 MEDIUM TOMATOES, PEELED, SEEDED, AND CHOPPED	

Soak the bread in the coconut milk for ½ hour.

Preheat the oven to 400°F. Grease a 10-inch pie pan.

In a bowl, mix the crabmeat, onions, salt, pepper, garlic, and lemon juice. Heat the olive oil in a skillet, add the crab mixture and sauté for 2 minutes. Stir in the chayote, tomatoes, and parsley, then lower the heat and simmer until all the liquid has evaporated. Mix in the bread and coconut milk. Remove from the heat and cool. Grind the mixture in a food processor or meat grinder until it resembles a coarse meal.

Beat the egg whites until stiff. Lightly beat the yolks. Fold the yolks into the whites, and add salt and black pepper to taste. Pour a layer of the egg mixture, about ½ inch deep, to cover the bottom of the dish. Mix ¼ cup of the eggs with the crabmeat and spoon the crab mixture over the egg layer. Top with the rest of the eggs. Decorate with the pepper rings. Place the tomato slices inside the pepper rings and an olive slice inside the tomato.

Bake until the top is golden, about 20 minutes.

Afro-Brazilian Okra Salad

Salada de Quiabo

4 TO 6 SERVINGS

OKRA IS A VERY POPULAR VEGETABLE in the northeast of Brazil. It was brought by slaves from the west coast of Africa and is a principal ingredient in many of the dishes associated with the Afro-Brazilian religious sects (Condomblé and Macumba). The following dish is often served with grilled fish.

SALAD:	VINAIGRETTE:
2½ POUNDS OKRA	2 ONIONS, FINELY CHOPPED
1 TEASPOON SALT	6 GARLIC CLOVES, MINCED
	¼ CUP OLIVE OIL
	¼ CUP RED WINE VINEGAR
	¼ TEASPOON SALT
	BLACK PEPPER
	2 TEASPOONS DIJON MUSTARD

Trim the ends of the okra and cut into ¼-inch slices. Place the okra and salt in a 4-quart pot with water to cover and bring to a boil. Cover, reduce the heat, and cook for 5 minutes. Drain the okra and place in a large bowl.

Mix the remaining ingredients in a blender until smooth and pour over the okra while it is still warm. Mix well and serve at room temperature.

Black-Eyed Peas *in* Coconut Milk

Feijão de Côco

4 SERVINGS

IN PERNAMBUCO, *feijão de coco* is usually served during lent along with Toasted Manioc Flour (page 40), white rice, and sautéed greens.

1 POUND BLACK-EYED PEAS	1 CUP COCONUT MILK
1 BAY LEAF	3 GREEN ONIONS, CHOPPED
2 TABLESPOONS OLIVE OIL	½ CUP CILANTRO LEAVES
5 GARLIC CLOVES, MINCED	SALT TO TASTE
1 MEDIUM ONION, MINCED	

Soak the black-eyed peas in water to cover for 6 hours or overnight. The following day drain the peas, removing any that float to top. Place in a pot, cover with fresh cold water, and bring to a boil over high heat. Reduce the heat, cover, and cook for 1½ to 2 hours or until tender. Let cool.

Drain the peas and place in a blender or food processor. Blend until the peas form a purée. Return to the pot and add the olive oil, garlic, onion, coconut milk, green onions, cilantro, and salt, stirring until the mixture returns to a boil.

Serve hot.

Spicy Greens

Efó

8 SERVINGS

EFÓ, A WORD OF AFRICAN ORIGIN, refers to a type of leafy green. In Bahia *efó* is prepared with a variety of greens the most popular being the leaves of *lingua de vaca* and *taioba*. Since these are not available outside of Brazil you can substitute spinach which comes closest to the *lingua-de-vaca*, the preferred type.

In the *Condomblé* religion, all of the gods and goddesses (*Orixás*) love to eat *efó* with the exception of *Oxalá* who detests spicy food. Bahians and other northeasterners consider this dish one of the best examples of their Afro-Brazilian cuisine.

1½ CUPS ROASTED, UNSALTED
  PEANUTS (12 OUNCES)
1 CUP ROASTED UNSALTED CASHEWS
  (8 OUNCES)
3½ CUPS DRIED SHRIMP
2 ONIONS, QUARTERED
4 GARLIC CLOVES
2 TABLESPOONS CHOPPED FRESH
  CILANTRO

1 POUND SPINACH, STEMMED,
  CHOPPED AND BLANCHED
1 CUP COCONUT MILK
¼ CUP OLIVE OIL
1 CUP PALM OIL
SALT AND BLACK PEPPER
1 JALAPEÑO PEPPER, SEEDED AND
  MINCED

In a meat grinder or food processor, grind the peanuts, cashews, dried shrimp, onions, garlic, and cilantro. Set aside.

Place the spinach in a saucepan with 1 cup water and bring to a boil. Add the coconut milk, olive oil, palm oil, salt, and pepper. Stir, reduce the heat and cook, stirring occasionally for 30 minutes or until the liquid has almost evaporated. Add salt to taste and the minced jalapeño. Mix well and serve hot with white rice.

NOTE: You can also substitute mustard greens for the *lingua-de-vaca*.

Brazilian Rice

Arroz Brasileiro
6 SERVINGS

THIS DISH IS A GREAT ACCOMPANIMENT to Bahian-Style Chicken (page 48), Bahian Shrimp and Bread Pudding (page 64-5), Bahian Fish Ragout (page 60), Haussa-Style Rice (page 74), or any grilled fish, poultry, or meat.

1 TEASPOON SALT	2 CUPS LONG-GRAIN RICE
2 TABLESPOONS OLIVE OIL, LARD,	2 MEDIUM ONIONS, DICED
BACON FAT OR MARGARINE	1 MEDIUM TOMATO, FINELY CHOPPED
(NOT BUTTER)	

Bring 5 cups of water to a boil with the salt.

Heat the olive oil in a medium skillet. Sauté the rice with the onions, stirring with a wooden spoon until the onions are golden and the rice is lightly browned, about 10 minutes. Stir in the tomato and remove from the heat. Slowly pour the boiling water over the rice mixture to avoid splattering. Stir once or twice; return to the heat and bring to a boil. When the mixture boils, cover and reduce the heat to a simmer. Cook for 25 minutes or until all the water is absorbed. Remove from the heat, uncover, and let the steam evaporate. Serve hot.

Haussá-Style Rice

Arroz-de-Hauçá
8 TO 10 SERVINGS

THE HAUSSÁ ARE NORTHERN NIGERIA'S largest ethnic group. They have long been good farmers, who cultivate rice as well as other grains. Slaves captured by the Haussá most likely introduced this dish in Brazil. Remember to soak the dried beef overnight for at least 6 hours to remove the salt so that it's ready for cooking the following day.

I first tasted this dish in the early 1960s while living in Salvador, Bahia at the home of Jorge Amado and Zelia Gattis. Since that time I have prepared it many times for family and friends. This recipe is the one Jorge and Zelia's cook prepared for me many years ago. *Arroz-de-Hauçá* was one of the favorite dishes of Brazilian novelist Jorge Amado. In fact, in many of his novels he depicts characters enjoying this dish of African origin.

DRIED BEEF:
2 POUNDS BRAZILIAN DRIED BEEF
2 TABLESPOONS OLIVE OIL
2 TABLESPOONS PALM OIL
1 LARGE ONION, THINLY SLICED
1 CUP COCONUT MILK

RICE:
¼ CUP OLIVE OIL
3 GARLIC CLOVES, MINCED
1 LARGE ONION, MINCED
4½ CUPS RICE
8 CUPS BOILING WATER
1 CUP COCONUT MILK

SHRIMP:
1 TABLESPOON OLIVE OIL
2 TABLESPOONS PALM OIL
1 LARGE ONION, MINCED
1 POUND LARGE FRESH SHRIMP
 (SEE NOTE)
1 CUP COCONUT MILK

SAUCE:
1 LARGE ONION, MINCED
1 LARGE TOMATO, PEELED
 AND SEEDED
1 CUP DRIED SHRIMP
2 TABLESPOONS OLIVE OIL
2 TABLESPOONS PALM OIL
1 TABLESPOON RED PEPPER FLAKES
1 TABLESPOON LEMON JUICE

FOR THE BEEF: Soak the beef for at least 6 hours or overnight to remove the salt. The following day remove all the fat and cut into 1-inch cubes. Place the cubes in a pot with water to cover. Bring to a boil and cook for 10 minutes; drain. Heat the olive oil and palm oil in a skillet and sauté the onion until translucent. Add the dried beef and coconut milk and continue to cook until the liquid has evaporated. Set aside.

FOR THE RICE: Heat the olive oil in a large pot. Add the garlic and onion and sauté until the onion is translucent. Stir in the rice and boiling water. Cover and cook over low heat for 15 minutes. Add the coconut milk and continue cooking for 10 minutes. Remove from the heat and pour into a buttered springform pan; set aside.

FOR THE SHRIMP: Heat the olive oil and the palm oil in a skillet and sauté the onion until it is translucent. Add the shrimp and the coconut milk and simmer until the shrimp is pink, about 5 minutes. Set aside.

FOR THE SAUCE: Place the onion in a food processor along with the tomato and dried shrimp. Pulse until the mixture resembles a purée. Heat the olive oil and palm oil in a skillet and add the shrimp mixture, the red pepper flakes, and lemon juice. Simmer for 10 minutes. Set aside.

TO SERVE: Invert the rice mold onto a platter. Place the shrimp sauce in the center of the rice mold and surround the mold with the beef mixture. Serve with the sauce on the side.

NOTE: Since the large whole dried shrimp that you can find in Brazil do not exist in the U.S. I have substituted large fresh shrimp. Some cooks add the sauce to the shrimp mixture instead of serving it on the side.

Broccoli Rice

Arroz de Brócolos

4 SERVINGS

BROCCOLI RICE IS A DISH FROM CEARÁ that is often served with a leg of goat marinated in red wine and cooked potatoes. This dish is quick and easy to prepare.

3 TABLESPOONS OF OLIVE OIL	1 TEASPOON SALT
3 GARLIC CLOVES, MINCED	3 CUPS COOKED WHITE RICE
1 MEDIUM ONION, MINCED	
1 BUNCH BROCCOLI, FLORETS ONLY, CHOPPED	

In a large skillet heat the olive oil and sauté the garlic and onion until soft. Add the broccoli, cover and cook, stirring occasionally until just tender, about 3 minutes. Add the salt and rice, and stir until the rice is hot.

Serve immediately.

Maria Isabel Rice

Arroz Maria Isabel

4 SERVINGS

MARIA ISABEL RICE is a very common dish eaten in the *sertão* (backlands) of Pernambuco and usually accompanies *Paçoca de Carne* (page 56).

2 POUNDS DRIED BRAZILIAN BEEF	1 TABLESPOON MINCED FRESH
½ CUP BUTTER	CILANTRO
1 ONION, JULIENNED	1 TEASPOON GROUND CUMIN
3 GARLIC CLOVES, MINCED	SALT
	1½ CUPS RICE

Soak the beef in cold water for 6 hours or overnight to remove the salt, changing the water at least twice. Cut the beef into cubes removing all the fat.

Heat the butter in a large skillet over medium low heat. Add the onion and garlic, stirring for 3 minutes. Add the beef and soaking water to barely cover and cook until the beef is tender, about 20 minutes. Stir in the cilantro, cumin, and salt to taste. Add the rice and 2 cups water. Cover and cook for another 20 minutes over medium heat. Cook until rice resembles risotto.

NOTE: Many cooks add a few drops of Tabasco or some *malagueta* pepper to the dish when the water and rice are added.

Coconut Cookies

Doces de Espécie
MAKES 12 COOKIES

THESE SWEETS, ALONG WITH MANY EGG-BASED DESSERTS, were introduced to the Iberian Peninsula by the Moors during their 800 years of occupation. The Portuguese nuns brought these desserts to the Northeast in the sixteenth century. With the arrival of slaves from Africa to work the sugar plantations, came coconut, which was added to these cookies. They soon became a favorite and are still served at many parties in the city of Alcântara, Maranhão as well as other parts of the northeast.

COCONUT FILLING:	DOUGH:
3 CUPS FRESHLY GRATED OR FROZEN UNSWEETENED COCONUT	2 CUPS FLOUR
	5 TABLESPOONS VEGETABLE OIL
2 CUPS SUGAR	¼ TEASPOON SALT

FOR THE FILLING: In a medium pot place the coconut, sugar, and 1 cup water over high heat and stir continuously until the sugar melts and begins to boil. Reduce the heat to medium and cook, stirring constantly until the mixture becomes a creamy paste. Remove from the heat and pour onto a buttered dish to cool.

FOR THE DOUGH: Preheat the oven to 350°F. Lightly dust a cookie sheet with flour.

Place the flour in a large bowl and make a well in the center. Add the oil, salt, and ½ cup water, and mix well until a stiff dough forms. Divide the dough in half and roll out one half on a floured surface. With a 3-inch cutter cut 12 circles. Roll out the remaining dough and cut into strips ½ inch thick in diameter and 4 inches long.

Place a teaspoon of coconut filling in the center of each circle. Crisscross 6 strips of dough over the coconut filling forming a lattice. Tuck the edges of the strips under the disk to seal. Place the cookies on the floured baking sheet and bake for 20 minutes or until golden. Remove from the oven and let cool for 10 minutes.

Arrange decoratively on a platter and serve.

Dreams

Sonhos

MAKES ABOUT 30

I FIRST TASTED THIS WONDERFUL DESSERT in Bahia in 1960, and it remains one of my favorites. *Sonhos* are enjoyed both in Brazil and Portugal during the Christmas holidays.

1 CUP FLOUR	2 TABLESPOONS BUTTER
2 TEASPOONS BAKING POWDER	2 EGGS, SEPARATED
¼ TEASPOON SALT	¼ CUP CHOPPED BRAZIL NUTS
1 (14-OUNCE) CAN SWEETENED	(1½ OUNCES)
CONDENSED MILK	¼ CUP WHOLE MILK

Preheat the oven to 400°F. Grease a miniature muffin tin.

Sift the flour, baking powder, and salt into a small bowl. Heat the condensed milk with the butter in a medium-size pot. When the mixture is hot, add the dry ingredients all at once, stirring rapidly. Reduce the heat to low, cook for 5 minutes, stirring constantly. Cool the mixture for 5 minutes.

Beat the egg whites until stiff peaks form. Beat the egg yolks, then fold in the whites. Add the nuts, milk, and condensed milk mixture. Spoon into the prepared tins, filling each three-quarters full. Bake for 8 minutes. Reduce the heat to 300°F and bake for another 8 minutes.

NOTE: For a beautiful presentation, sprinkle the cooled *sonhos* with powdered sugar.

Mother-in-Law's Eyes

Olhos de Sogra

4 TO 6 SERVINGS

IN BRAZIL THERE ARE SEVERAL DESSERTS with imaginative and funny names. This dessert is yet another example of this culinary humor. When this dessert is prepared the stuffed prune with the clove in the center resembles an eye. It is thought that it is reminiscent of a mother-in-law watching her daughter-in-law.

1 CUP SUGAR	1 POUND LARGE PITTED PRUNES
1 CUP FRESH OR FROZEN GRATED	WHOLE CLOVES FOR GARNISH
COCONUT	CONFECTIONER SUGAR FOR ROLLING
2 EGG YOLKS	

Place the sugar and 1 cup water in a saucepan over low heat. Add the grated coconut and the egg yolks. Cook slowly, stirring from time to time, until the mixture thickens, about 10 minutes. Remove from the heat and cool slightly.

Make a slit lengthwise along the top of the pitted prunes and open slightly to form a boat shape. Stuff each prune with 1 teaspoon of the coconut mixture. Let the filling cover the top of the prune. Decorate with 1 clove in the center of each prune to form the pupil of the eye. Roll the boat-shaped prunes in the powdered sugar and place on a serving tray. Serve with coffee.

Golden Coconut Cupcakes

Quindins
MAKES 12 CUPCAKES

LEGEND HAS IT THAT PORTUGUESE NUNS, who were well known for their tasty egg custards, brought this recipe with them to Brazil. Coconut, which is not native to Portugal, was added later by the African slaves.

Quindins are very sweet cupcakes that were popular during slavery times in the master's house on plantations in the northeast of Brazil. The cakes were served at family dinners and elaborate parties. Baked in individual pastry or muffin tins, they are then inverted and served in little silver paper cups for a festive touch. As the *quindins* cook the coconut rises to the top and forms a light brown crust. When inverted, the coconut is on the bottom and the yolks form a golden dome on top.

This recipe can be doubled and baked in an angel food cake or Bundt pan. It is then called a *quindão*, which means "big cupcake."

1 STICK BUTTER PLUS ADDITIONAL MELTED BUTTER FOR GREASING TINS	15 EGG YOLKS
	1 WHOLE EGG
1½ CUPS EXTRA FINE SUGAR, PLUS ADDITIONAL FOR DUSTING TINS	1½ CUPS FRESH OR FROZEN UNSWEETENED GRATED COCONUT

Preheat the oven to 350°F. Using a pastry brush, grease a muffin tin with melted butter and dust with sugar.

Beat the sugar and butter in a medium-size mixing bowl until fluffy. Add the egg yolks and the whole egg, 1 at a time, beating well after each addition. Fold in the coconut and mix gently just to incorporate.

Fill the tins almost to the top with the custard. Set the muffin tin in a baking pan. Pour hot water into the pan to a depth of 1 inch to make a bain-marie. Bake the *quindims* for about 35 minutes or until they are firm and slightly golden. Cool in muffin tin for 10 minutes on a rack and then chill for at least 4 hours or overnight. Remove from the tins by running a knife around each custard to loosen. Invert onto a plate and place in silver paper cups or arrange on a serving dish.

Souza Leão Cake

Bolo Souza Leão
20 SERVINGS

SOUZA LEÃO CAKE IS ONE OF THE MOST FAMOUS CAKES in the Northeast, and in all of Brazil for that matter. It is named after an old Pernambuco family of sugarcane planters who owned five plantations. There are several recipes for this cake with slight variations in the amount of ingredients and, at times, the introduction of new ingredients depending on which plantation it came from.

This recipe is very similar to the original cake that made the family's name famous throughout Brazil.

4½ CUPS SUGAR	3 CUPS COCONUT MILK
2 CUPS BUTTER	2 TEASPOONS GROUND CINNAMON
1 TEASPOON SALT	1 TEASPOON GROUND CLOVES
2½ CUPS FINE MANIOC FLOUR	1 TEASPOON ANISEED
16 EGG YOLKS	

Preheat the oven to 425°F. Butter a 10-inch tube cake pan and dust with flour.

Place the sugar and 2 cups cold water in a pan over high heat. Stir constantly until the sugar is dissolved and reaches the fine thread stage (235°F). Remove from the heat and stir in the butter and salt. Set aside to cool.

Place the manioc flour in a large bowl and add the egg yolks one by one, stirring well after each addition, alternating with the coconut milk. Add the cooled sugar syrup and strain through a sieve 3 times. Add the cinnamon, cloves, and aniseed.

Pour the batter into the prepared pan and place in a bain-marie (a larger baking pan filled with 1-inch of hot water). Bake for 50 to 60 minutes until golden brown and a toothpick comes out clean.

Place on cake rack and cool for 1 hour. Invert onto a serving plate.

NOTE: To serve, the cake can be drizzled with molasses and sprinkled with grated coconut.

BRAZIL | A CULINARY JOURNEY

Jelly Roll Cake

Bolo de Rolo

MAKES 60 THIN SLICES

THIS CAKE, WITH A THIN FILLING OF GUAVA JELLY, is as famous as the Souza Leão Cake but a little more difficult to prepare. Jelly roll cake is very similar to a famous cake in Goa, influenced by the Portuguese, called *bibinca de sete folhas* made with seven layers rather than as a jelly roll. This cake is usually served at receptions or other large gatherings.

CAKE:	FILLING:
5 STICKS BUTTER, AT ROOM TEMPERATURE	1½ CUPS GUAVA JELLY, MELTED
2¾ CUPS SUGAR	TOPPING:
8 EGGS, SEPARATED	6 TABLESPOONS GRANULATED SUGAR
4 CUPS FLOUR	POWDERED SUGAR, FOR SPRINKLING

FOR THE CAKE: Preheat the oven to 400°F. Grease a 12 x 18-inch baking sheet.

Beat the butter with an electric mixer, on high, until fluffy. Add the sugar a little at a time and beat for 5 minutes. Add the yolks one at a time, and beat until the mixture is light and creamy. Reduce the speed and add the flour slowly until it is well mixed and the batter is creamy and smooth.

Beat the egg whites until stiff and fold into the batter with a rubber spatula. Spread 1 cup of batter over the prepared baking sheet, smoothing with a spatula. Bake for 4 minutes. Do not let the dough brown. Carefully turn the layer out onto a kitchen towel sprinkled with granulated sugar. Brush a thin layer of guava jelly over the cake and using the cloth, immediately roll up jelly roll-style beginning with one of the short sides.

Wash the baking sheet, dry, and grease again. Repeat the process with layers until all the batter has been used. You should have at least 8 rolls. Let the cakes cool. Slice thinly and place on a platter. Sprinkle with sugar and serve.

Corn Pudding

Canjica de Milho Verde

6 TO 8 SERVINGS

IN BAHIA, *canjica* is served as part of St. John's Day festivities on June 24. St. John's is also the day for the feast of corn and a variety of corn dishes are prepared to celebrate. In northern Brazil, where the dish is called *mungunzá*, it is made with hominy and roasted peanuts. In São Paulo and Minas Gerais, as well as Bahia, *canjica* is made with freshly grated corn and called *chá-de-burro*, which translates as "donkey's tea."

8 EARS CORN, HUSKED	1 TABLESPOON BUTTER
1 (14-OUNCE) CAN COCONUT MILK	GROUND CINNAMON
¼ TEASPOON SALT	
5 TABLESPOONS SUGAR	

With a sharp knife, cut the kernels from each cob into a medium-size bowl. Using the dull side of the knife, scrape the pulp from the cobs into the bowl. Place the corn in a blender or food processor with 1 cup of the coconut milk and grind to a smooth pulp. Strain through a coarse strainer into a bowl, using the back of a wooden spoon to press the pulp through the strainer. Add the salt, sugar, butter, and remaining coconut milk. Place in a medium-size pot and cook over low heat, stirring constantly until the mixture thickens. When it is thick enough to coat the back of a spoon, remove from the heat and cool.

Pour the mixture into a shallow 1-quart dish and refrigerate. Before serving, place a doily on the pudding and sprinkle cinnamon over top. Remove the doily and serve.

Rum Cocktail

Caipirinha

4 SERVINGS

CAIPIRINHAS ARE BRAZIL'S signature cocktail. The name itself is the diminutive of *caipira*, which is more or less equivalent to a "hillbilly" from the state of São Paulo. Actually, the drink originated farther to the north in sugarcane-growing regions. *Cachaça, caipirinha's* chief ingredient, is, in fact, alcohol distilled from sugarcane juice. This beverage, long associated with the lower classes, has become the national liquor. Today, members of the middle and upper classes regularly consume *cachaça*, most often in *caipirinhas* and *batidas*.

Cachaça is available outside of Brazil, but not in every city. Check your local liquor store as many are importing this liquor today. If not available, white rum is a good substitute, although it's distilled from molasses (a sugarcane extract).

2 TABLESPOONS SUGAR	1 CUP *CACHAÇA* OR WHITE RUM
JUICE OF 2 LIMES, RINDS RESERVED	1 CUP CRUSHED ICE

In a cocktail shaker combine the sugar, lime juice, *cachaça*, and crushed ice, shake well. Cut the rinds into pieces and divide among 4 (8-ounce) glasses. Pour the *caipirinhas* over the rinds, stir and serve.

Hot Chocolate *with* Egg Yolks

Chocolate com Gemas
MAKES 4 TO 6 CUPS

IN THE LATE 1600S, cacao became one of Brazil's main exports and by the 1920s Brazil ranked second in the world as an exporter of cacao products. This drink grew out of the Brazilians' love for chocolate. Jorge Amado documented this love in several of his novels, which were set in the cacao-growing region of the state of Bahia.

2 (2-OUNCE) SQUARES UNSWEETENED CHOCOLATE	2 EGG YOLKS
	2 TABLESPOONS SUGAR
1 QUART WHOLE MILK	WHIPPED CREAM FOR GARNISH

Place the chocolate in a medium-sized pot over low heat and gradually add the milk. Continue cooking until the chocolate has melted. Do not let the mixture boil. Remove from the heat.

Beat the egg yolks with the sugar until frothy and slowly add to the chocolate mixture, mixing well. Return the pot to the heat and bring to a boil to scald the milk. Taste and add more sugar if desired. Remove from heat and serve hot with the whipped cream.

Southeastern Cuisine

poultry

beef

bananas

São Paulo

Rio de Janeiro

Minas Gerais

Espírito Santo

pizza

coconut palms

The four states that comprise the southeastern region are from north to south, Minas Gerais, Espírito Santo, Rio de Janeiro, and São Paulo. Without a doubt the names of the latter two states are the most recognizable to foreigners. This is especially true because Rio de Janeiro and São Paulo are also the names of these two states' capital cities, as well as Brazil's most populous urban centers.

A Brazilian born and raised in the city of Rio is called a *Carioca*, a designation of Tupi-Guarani Indian origin meaning "home of the newcomer's," the latter being, of course, the Portuguese settlers. In the realm of the city's traditional cuisine, *Feijoada Carioca* (Carioca Bean Stew) is a favorite throughout Brazil. The

Rio version differs from *Feijoada Bahiana* in that it includes black beans rather than brown mulatto beans. The state of Rio de Janeiro and especially its cosmopolitan capital city is home to a plethora of ethnically diverse dishes and foods of indigenous origin that have converged to characterize its traditional cuisine.

The cuisine of the state of São Paulo, whose capital is Brazil's most populous and most industrialized city, has been influenced by waves of migrants from other regions of the country and from throughout the world. In the city of São Paulo's diverse neighborhoods, one finds Italian, German, Japanese, and other ethnic restaurants. The city's cuisine is truly international. Throughout the state there are also restaurants that specialize in dishes from Pernambuco, Bahia, Minas Gerais, and other parts of Brazil. Pizza has become a favorite food, especially in São Paulo, but rice and bean dishes continue to be favorites in the interior of the state.

Minas Gerais translates as "general mines," and the first settlers went there in search of gold and precious stones. These miners helped determine the nature of early foods and eating habits. The journey from the coast was long and arduous and they made do with whatever game they came upon, deer, birds, and even snakes. Miners also fished in the streams and rivers, and collected honey, hearts of palm and wild vegetables.

By the nineteenth century, because mining for gold and other precious ores and stones had ceased to be profitable sources of income, many miners turned to farming, ranching, and sugarcane cultivation, all of which effected some changes in culinary habits. From the interior of the state of Minais Gerais, Vila de Sabra and surrounding areas beans, corn, rice, sugarcane, cattle, and freshwater fish, were brought in. Sought after fruits, such as apples, peaches, and grapes were originally introduced by the Portuguese and were cultivated in the Vila Nova do Rainha area. From the Tiradentes area, came cattle and cheese. The cattle ranching provided beef, which they sun-dried, salted, and cut into slabs known as *carne-de-sol*. Inhabitants of the state also salted and smoked cuts of pork. Lard is still used to prepare *paçoca* (manioc flour sautéed in fat). Generally, cattle ranchers did not drink milk, but they did make cheese, today known as *queijo de minas*, now a favorite nationwide that is eaten at breakfast as well as for dessert.

Belo Horizonte (beautiful horizon), the capital of Minas Gerais, is true to its name. The Pampula Chapel, designed by Oscar Niemeyer, contains the famous *Via Sacra* painted by Portinari. Minas Gerais is also famous for its *couve à Mineira* (Mineira-style collards) and *paçoca de carnes seca* (sun-dried beef with manioc flour). The daily fare of the Minas Gerais table is traditionally the same as it was at the turn of the century, and varies little throughout the state. The main dishes continue to be beans, corn or manioc meal mush, rice, pork loin, pork sausage, pork cracklings, beef—fresh or dried, chicken, and collard greens.

Espirito Santo, which lies on the coast just north of Rio de Janeiro and south of the state of Bahia is known as the land of the *capixaba*. The term *capixaba* is etymologically linked to *roçado*, which in the language of the Tupi Indians means "small property" or "corn ranch." This designation was applied because of the many ways corn is prepared. The combination of the cuisine of the *Tupi* and the Portuguese, in some cases with a significant African influence, has resulted in dishes that have become regional favorites, especially *torta* (torte) and the *moqueca capixaba* (capixaba stew). The word *moqueca* derives from *muke-ka*, from the Kimbundo language of Angola, the former Portuguese colony in southwest Africa. Moqueca is a stew made with fresh or saltwater fish. The *moqueca* of Espirito Santo differs from the *moqueca de camarão* of Bahia. It is prepared with olive oil and cooked in a clay pot. The Bahian version of the dish has as ingredients palm oil and coconut milk, and is prepared in a skillet.

Torta and the *moqueca* are dishes that symbolize the cultural formation of the *capixaba* people, the product of the mixture of the Portuguese, Indian, and African culinary influences. The transplanted Portuguese and the Africans greatly influenced the native Indians' cuisine by introducing hot sauces, oils, and other seasonings, and by cooking in clay pots over hot coals.

Capixaba cuisine, just like Brazilian cuisine, was born with the Indians. The technique of preparing manioc flour or *farinha* with its derivatives of tapioca, tapioca cake and manioc purée, and the use of the plantain, baked, fried, boiled, or mashed with coconut, are all influences not withstanding, as well as a number of other Brazilian dishes, that originated in the food cultures of the indigenous peoples.

Heart *of* Palm Pastries

Pastéis de Palmito
MAKES 60 PASTRIES

HEART OF PALM PASTRIES are enjoyed by all Paulistas, the people of São Paulo. They are served, along with the typical plate of beans and rice, in the finest restaurants. One can also find them in open air markets, fried on the spot for hungry shoppers.

FILLING:
2 TABLESPOONS BUTTER
½ CUP MINCED ONION
1 (7¾-OUNCE) CAN PALM HEARTS,
   DRAINED AND CHOPPED
1 TABLESPOON FLOUR
1 CUP WHOLE MILK
1 TEASPOON SALT
¼ TEASPOON BLACK PEPPER

10 PITTED BLACK OLIVES, CHOPPED

DOUGH:
5 CUPS FLOUR
1 TABLESPOON SALT
1½ TEASPOONS SUGAR
5 TABLESPOONS LIGHT BRANDY
VEGETABLE OIL FOR FRYING

FOR THE FILLING: Melt the butter in a medium-size saucepan over medium heat. Add the onions and stir frequently until lightly golden. Stir in the palm hearts and cook for another 5 minutes. Meanwhile, dissolve the flour in the milk and add it to the palm heart mixture, stirring constantly to keep lumps from forming. Cook until the mixture thickens, then remove from the heat. Season with the salt and black pepper, stir in the olives, and set aside.

FOR THE DOUGH: Pour the flour into a large bowl. Make a well in the center and add the salt, sugar, and brandy. Mix well. Add 1½ cups water, a little at a time, mixing well after each addition, until the dough comes together in a ball.

Place the dough on a floured surface and knead until smooth. Roll the dough ¼ inch thick and cut into 3-inch circles. Place a teaspoon of filling in the center of each circle. Dampen the edges with water and fold over to form a half circle. Press the edges together with the tines of a fork. Repeat until all the circles are used. Pour about 2 cups of vegetable oil into a pot for deep frying, heating oil to 350°F. Fry the pastries a few at a time until golden on both sides, about 3 minutes. Remove and drain on paper towels.

Serve warm or at room temperature.

Chicken Pastries

Empadinhas de Galinha

MAKES 1 DOZEN PASTRIES

MANY PEOPLE BELIEVE that *empadinhas* originated in Brazil, but a 1692 Portuguese cookbook including recipes for *empadinhas* reveals that they were brought to Brazil by the Portuguese. They were then adapted to the ingredients available in South America and have become a staple of Brazilian cuisine. *Empadinhas* and the *pastel* fit into the category of *salgado*, which literally means "salty," but includes any appetizers or finger foods served with drinks before a meal. *Empadinha* dough uses shortening and eggs and is always baked, while *pastel* dough is similar to pie pastry and can be baked or fried. Serve these pastries as part of a buffet with other finger foods. The filling should be prepared one day in advance.

MARINADE:	1 TABLESPOON BUTTER OR
1 MEDIUM ONION, CHOPPED	MARGARINE
JUICE OF 1 LEMON	¼ CUP TOMATO SAUCE
¼ CUP WHITE VINEGAR	2 TABLESPOONS CORNSTARCH
4 FRESH MINT LEAVES	3 CUPS WHOLE MILK
1 TEASPOON DRIED SAVORY	2 EGG YOLKS, LIGHTLY BEATEN
¼ CUP CHOPPED FRESH PARSLEY	12 BLACK OLIVES
¼ CUP OLIVE OIL	3 HARD-BOILED EGGS, QUARTERED
2 GARLIC CLOVES, CHOPPED	1 EGG, LIGHTLY BEATEN
1 TEASPOON SALT	
1 TEASPOON WHOLE CORIANDER	PASTRY:
SEEDS	2½ CUPS FLOUR
½ TEASPOON BLACK PEPPER	¼ CUP BUTTER
	¼ CUP LARD OR SHORTENING
	½ TEASPOON SALT
FILLING:	3 EGG YOLKS
6 BONELESS SKINLESS CHICKEN	¼ CUP WHOLE MILK
THIGHS	

FOR THE MARINADE: Mix all the ingredients in a blender or food processor until a purée forms. Set aside.

FOR THE FILLING: Remove any fat from the chicken and place in a nonreactive bowl. Pour ½ cup marinade over chicken. Cover and refrigerate overnight, turning occasionally.

The following day, preheat the oven to 350°F and grease muffin tins. Melt the butter in a large skillet over medium-high heat and quickly brown the chicken on all sides. Cover, reduce the heat, and cook for 5 minutes, turning once. Add the remaining marinade and continue cooking for 5 minutes. Add the tomato sauce and ⅓ cup water. Mix well and cook until the chicken is tender, about 10 minutes. Remove the chicken from the sauce and let cool. Shred the chicken and set aside. Mix the cornstarch with ⅓ cup of the milk and add it to the sauce in the skillet. Stir until smooth. Heat the sauce over low heat until it begins to thicken, then slowly add the remaining 2⅔ cups milk, stirring continuously, until the sauce is smooth. Remove the skillet from heat. Beat the egg yolks with 2 tablespoons of the warm sauce. Pour the egg yolk mixture back into the skillet over low heat. Cook the mixture, stirring occasionally, for about 5 minutes. Add the chicken, mix well, and taste for seasonings.

FOR THE PASTRY: Put the flour into a large bowl. Melt the butter and lard together and add them to the flour, mixing until crumbly. In another mixing bowl, combine the salt and 1 tablespoon water. Add the egg yolks one at a time. Fold the egg mixture into the flour and add the milk. Mix well and shape into a ball. Cover and set aside for 1 hour. Meanwhile prepare the filling.

Uncover the pastry and roll out on floured board a thinly as possible, about ⅛ inch thick. Cut rounds about 1 inch larger than the muffin tins. Press into the tins and up the sides. Fill the tins three-quarters full with filling. Top with an olive and a piece of hard-boiled egg. Cut a round of dough ½-inch larger than the diameter of the top of the tin. Press the edges together to seal with your fingers or the tines of a fork dipped in water. Brush each pastry with the beaten egg. Bake for 20 to 30 minutes. Cool, and serve as part of a buffet or as a light lunch with a green salad.

Cornmeal *and* Beef Pastries

Pastéis de Farinha de Milho e Bife

MAKES 25 TO 30 PASTRIES

THESE APPETIZERS ARE FOUND throughout the state of São Paulo and served at birthday, anniversary, and wedding parties. The unique dough is made from a mixture of corn flour and manioc flour. The use of manioc flour could very well be a native Indian influence.

FILLING:
- 2 TABLESPOONS VEGETABLE OIL
- 2 GARLIC CLOVES, MINCED
- 1 SMALL ONION, MINCED
- 8 OUNCES GROUND BEEF
- 2 ROMA TOMATOES, SEEDED AND CHOPPED
- 2 TABLESPOONS MINCED GREEN BELL PEPPER
- 1 TEASPOON SALT
- ½ TEASPOON BLACK PEPPER
- 1 TABLESPOON FLOUR
- 1 EGG, HARD-BOILED AND CHOPPED
- 1 TABLESPOON CHOPPED FRESH PARSLEY
- 1 TABLESPOON CHOPPED FRESH CILANTRO
- 10 PIMENTO-STUFFED GREEN OLIVES

DOUGH:
- 1 CUP CORN MEAL (NOT STONEGROUND)
- 1 CUP MANIOC FLOUR
- 1 CUP HOT WATER
- 1 TEASPOON SALT
- 1 EGG YOLK
- 1 WHOLE EGG
- VEGETABLE OIL FOR FRYING

FOR THE FILLING: Heat the oil in a skillet over high heat. Add the garlic and onion and sauté until the onion is translucent and soft. Add the ground beef and sauté, stirring constantly until the beef is browned. Add the tomatoes, green peppers, and ½ cup water, season with the salt and black pepper, and cook for another 5 minutes. Sprinkle the flour over the meat mixture and mix well. Mix in the hard-boiled egg, parsley, cilantro, and olives, remove from heat and set aside.

FOR THE DOUGH: Place the corn and manioc flours in a large bowl. Add the hot water and salt and mix until a thick mush forms. Add the yolk and whole egg and knead until the dough is smooth and elastic. Place ¼ of the dough between 2 pieces of plastic wrap and roll out to ¼-inch thickness. Cut out 3-inch circles with a round cookie cutter. Place a heaping teaspoon of filling on each circle. Fold the dough over to form a half circle and press to seal.

Heat 2 inches of oil in a deep pot or fryer to 350°F. Fry the pastries, a few at a time, turning until golden on both sides. Remove and drain on paper towels.

Serve warm or at room temperature.

Delicate Soup

Sopa Delicada

4 TO 6 SERVINGS

MANY PORTUGUESE JEWS who were expulsed from Portugal during the Inquisition fled to Brazil and brought with them many traditional dishes including *Sopa Delicada*. They continued to make this traditional potato dumpling soup but, over the decades it has undergone some modifications, and today some moderate Jews even include the use of ham.

BROTH:	½ CUP GRATED PARMESAN CHEESE
2 QUARTS BEEF BOUILLON	(2 OUNCES)
1 LARGE CARROT, PEELED AND	3 EGGS, SEPARATED
CHOPPED	3 TABLESPOONS GROUND HAM
4 SPRIGS PARSLEY	(GROUND IN THE FOOD PROCESSOR)
	2 TABLESPOONS BUTTER
POTATO BALLS:	¼ TEASPOON GROUND NUTMEG
2 POUNDS WHITE POTATOES	1 CUP FLOUR
2 TEASPOONS SALT	VEGETABLE OIL FOR FRYING

FOR THE BROTH: Bring the bouillon, carrot, and parsley to a boil in a large pot and cook for 10 minutes.

FOR THE POTATO BALLS: Place the potatoes in a large pot of cold water with 1 teaspoon of salt and cook for 20 minutes or until the potatoes are tender. Cool the potatoes for 5 minutes, then peel, and push through a strainer or ricer, or mash with a fork. While warm, add ¼ cup of the Parmesan cheese, the egg yolks, ham, butter, nutmeg, and remaining 1 teaspoon of salt. Mix well.

In a 1-quart pot, heat 2 inches of oil to 350°F. Make balls the size of walnuts with the mashed potato, roll them in the flour and fry them in the hot oil. When golden brown, remove and place on a rack or absorbent paper. Remove the carrots and parsley from the stock and bring the stock to a boil. Add the potato balls, reduce the heat, and simmer for 3 to 5 minutes. Pour into a soup tureen and sprinkle with ¼ cup or more of the Parmesan cheese. Serve immediately.

Chicken *with* Okra

Frango com Quiabo

4 TO 6 SERVINGS

IN MINAS GERAIS this dish is known as *Xi com Angu*. In the past when men wanted to get together at night to play cards or other games and drink, they would tell their wives that "Chico has invited us to eat chicken with okra." When they arrived home in the wee hours of the morning to complaining wives they would say "Instead of Chico preparing a chicken he prepared a rooster with okra, and everyone knows it takes longer to prepare a rooster than a chicken. That's why it took so long." Hence the dish became known as *Xi com Angu*, or *Xi* with mush (Xi is a nickname for Chico). It is said that the dish was the favorite of the former Brazilian President Juscelino Kubitschek.

1 (3-POUND) CHICKEN OR EQUIVALENT WEIGHT IN BREASTS AND/OR THIGHS	2 GARLIC CLOVES, MINCED
JUICE OF 1 LEMON	2 TABLESPOONS VEGETABLE OIL
1½ ONIONS, MINCED	1 POUND TOMATOES, SEEDED AND CHOPPED
½ CUP MINCED FRESH CILANTRO	1 POUND OKRA, TRIMMED AND CHOPPED
SALT AND BLACK PEPPER	

Cut the chicken into 8 pieces, rinse, and rub with the lemon juice. Combine one third of the minced onion, the cilantro, salt and black pepper, and garlic. Toss the chicken with the onion mixture and let sit for 15 minutes. Heat the oil in a large skillet and cook chicken pieces until golden brown on all sides. Add the tomato and remaining onion, cover and simmer for 10 minutes, adding a little water if the mixture dries out. Add the okra and cook without stirring for another 10 minutes. Serve on a platter with *Pirão* (page 140) on the side.

Shredded Beef *in* Tomato Sauce

Roupa-Velha
3 TO 4 SERVINGS

ROUPA-VELHA, LITERALLY "OLD CLOTHES," means leftover or hand-me-down. Thus, this dish is a wonderful way to use leftover grilled, roasted, or stewed beef.

1½ POUNDS LEFTOVER BEEF ROAST OR STEW	2 TABLESPOONS LEMON JUICE
½ TEASPOON HOT PEPPER SAUCE	1 TEASPOON SALT
2 POUNDS FRESH TOMATOES CHOPPED (8 ROMA TOMATOES)	1 SMALL ONION, CHOPPED
2 TABLESPOONS OLIVE OIL	1 TEASPOON WHITE PEPPER
	½ CUP BRANDY

Shred the meat and mix it with the pepper sauce in a large bowl. Set aside.

Place the tomatoes in a large pot with ¾ cup water, the olive oil, lemon juice, salt, onion, and white pepper and cook for 20 minutes or until the tomatoes are soft. Remove from the heat, cool and process in a food processor or blender until it forms a purée. Return the purée to the pot and bring to a boil. Add the brandy and remove from heat.

Mix the shredded beef with the tomato sauce and serve with white rice.

Beef Rolls

Bifes Enrolados
8 SERVINGS

BEEF IS THE MOST POPULAR MEAT in southeastern and southern Brazil. This recipe is enjoyed by Cariocas and Paulistas alike. Begin the preparation a day in advance because the meat has to marinate overnight.

2 POUNDS ROUND STEAK, VERY THINLY SLICED INTO 8 PIECES	8 HARD-BOILED EGG YOLKS
2 CLOVES GARLIC	1 TABLESPOON MUSTARD
1 TEASPOON SALT	6 TABLESPOONS BUTTER, SOFTENED
½ TEASPOON BLACK PEPPER	½ CUP CHOPPED BLACK OLIVES
1 CUP PORT	
½ POUND BOILED HAM, THINLY SLICED	

Pound the steaks with a mallet. Rub both sides with the garlic and sprinkle with the salt and black pepper. Place in a non-reactive container with the port and marinate for at least 6 hours or overnight.

The following day, remove the beef from the marinade, reserve the marinade, and cover each piece with a slice of ham. Mash the egg yolks with 3 tablespoons of the butter and the mustard and season to taste with salt and black pepper. Spread the mixture over each slice of ham and sprinkle the olives on top. Roll the steaks up lengthwise, cut into thirds and tie each roll securely on both ends with kitchen twine. Heat the remaining 3 tablespoons of butter and sauté the rolls until well browned on all sides. Add the reserved marinade to the pan. Cover and cook over medium heat for 5 minutes, then lower the heat and cook until the rolls are tender, about 2 hours. Add a little water to the marinade if it begins to dry out. Remove the rolls, place them on a serving platter, remove the strings and serve with the pan gravy. A good accompaniment to this dish is mashed potatoes and buttered peas.

NOTE: The hard-boiled egg whites may be used in a salad.

Brazilian Hash

Picadinho

8 TO 10 SERVINGS

THIS DISH CAME TO PORTUGAL by way of Iran and originally called for diced lamb with any of the following ingredients: eggplant, tomatoes, spinach, scallions, leeks, dill, lemon or quince. *Picadinho*, one of the most traditional *Carioca* dishes, and is served in many restaurants. In the sixteenth century, Sephardic Jews, many of whom were *conversos* (converts) or New Christians, left the Iberian Peninsula to settle in Brazil. Once introduced to Brazil, Sephardic cuisine underwent modifications because of the influence of new ingredients and the food cultures of the local Indians and slaves of African origin. Thus, although in Portugal, *picada de vaca*, the Sephardic precursor of *picadinho* includes mainly olives and eggs, in the northern Brazilian state of Bahia it is made with okra and chayote. Palm oil has taken the place of vegetable oil, and because the juices from the chayote and okra suffice, cooks do not usually add broth. *Farofa*, made with manioc flour, is now a common accompaniment to the Bahian variation. In southern Brazil, in the state of Rio Grande do Sul, Sephardic cooks added raisins and manioc flour. The Brazilian version of the recipe, unlike the Portuguese original, calls for tomatoes and green peppers.

Picadinho is the diminutive of *picado* and literally means "cut into very small pieces," the equivalent to dicing. Today, many cooks use ground beef because of its availability and convenience.

2 POUNDS ROUND STEAK	½ TEASPOON BLACK PEPPER
2 TABLESPOONS VEGETABLE OIL	1 TEASPOON DRIED OREGANO
1 LARGE ONION, CHOPPED	2 TABLESPOONS FLOUR
4 GARLIC CLOVES, MINCED	2 CUPS BEEF BOUILLON
2 GREEN BELL PEPPERS, SEEDED AND CHOPPED	2 CUPS WHITE RICE
2 LARGE TOMATOES, PEELED AND CHOPPED	5 EGGS, HARD-BOILED AND CHOPPED
2 TEASPOONS SALT	1 CUP PIMENTO-STUFFED GREEN OLIVES

Trim all the fat from the steak and cut into ¼-inch cubes or mince in a food processor (do not grind). Heat the oil in a large pot and sauté the onion and garlic. Add the green peppers and sauté for 1 minute more. Add the meat, stir well and continue sautéing just until the meat is no longer pink, but is not browned. Add the tomatoes, 1 teaspoon of the salt, the pepper, and oregano. Sprinkle the flour over the meat mixture, cook, stirring for 1 minute. Add the bouillon, mix well, then cover and simmer for 30 minutes.

In another medium-size pot bring 4 cups water and the remaining 1 teaspoon salt to a boil. Add the rice, stir, cover, and simmer for 20 minutes.

Place the rice in the center of a large deep platter. Pour the meat over the rice and garnish with eggs and olives.

NOTE: The egg yolks may be omitted if you prefer. It will not alter the taste of the original recipe.

Pumpkin and Dried Beef Torte

Bolo de Quibebe

8 SERVINGS

QUIBEBE COMES FROM THE INTERIOR of São Paulo. It is served on many buffet tables for anniversaries, parties, and other special occasions. The orange color of the pumpkin with the collard greens makes for a very colorful and tasty dish.

1 POUND DRIED BRAZILIAN BEEF	2 HEADS GARLIC, CLOVES PEELED,
5 POUNDS PUMPKIN OR BUTTERNUT	SEPARATED, AND CRUSHED
SQUASH, PEELED AND CUT INTO 2-	SALT AND BLACK PEPPER
INCH PIECES	1 TEASPOON CHOPPED FRESH BASIL
6 TABLESPOONS OLIVE OIL	1 BUNCH COLLARD GREENS, STEMMED
1 SMALL ONION, MINCED	AND FINELY CHOPPED

Rinse the dried beef, cover with water and soak for 6 hours or overnight in the refrigerator.

Preheat the oven to 400°F and grease a baking sheet.

Place the pumpkin on the prepared baking sheet and bake until soft, about 20 minutes. Remove from the oven and place in a colander. Let the pumpkin sit until all the liquid drains off. Put the pumpkin through a ricer or mash with a fork, removing all lumps. Place the purée in a pot with 2 tablespoons of the olive oil, half the onions, half the garlic, and the basil. Season with salt and pepper, and cook until quite dry.

Rinse the beef and place it in a pot with cold water to cover. Bring to a boil, then reduce the heat and simmer for 20 minutes, or until tender. Remove from the heat, drain and shred the meat, discarding any fat. In a large skillet heat 2 tablespoons of the olive oil. Add the remaining onions, half the remaining garlic, and the beef, and sauté until the onions are golden. Taste for salt, remove from the heat and set aside.

Heat the remaining 2 tablespoons in a medium-size pan and over high heat and add the remaining garlic and salt to taste. Sauté until soft and add the collard greens. Cook, stirring, until tender, about 15 minutes.

Line a springform pan with aluminum foil and grease the foil with olive oil. Spread half of the pumpkin on the bottom, cover with a layer of collard greens, then a layer of dried beef, and lastly the remaining pumpkin. Reduce the oven temperature to 350°F and bake for about 40 minutes or until firm. Turn out onto a platter and serve.

Espirito Santo Fish Ragout

Moqueca Capixaba

4 SERVINGS

THE *MOQUECA* FROM THE STATE of Espirito Santo differs from the *moqueca* prepared in the northeast. This dish uses olive oil instead of palm oil and does not use coconut milk. It is also served in a clay pot.

ANNATTO OIL:
2½ TABLESPOONS ANNATTO SEEDS
1 CUP VEGETABLE OIL

RAGOUT:
2 GARLIC CLOVES, CRUSHED
SALT
3 TABLESPOONS LIME OR LEMON JUICE
2 POUNDS FISH STEAKS (GROUPER, SEA
  BASS, OR SNAPPER)

3 TABLESPOONS OLIVE OIL
1 LARGE ONION, CHOPPED
4 LARGE TOMATOES, PEELED, SEEDED,
  AND CHOPPED
2 TABLESPOONS CHOPPED GREEN
  ONIONS
2 TABLESPOONS CHOPPED FRESH
  CILANTRO

FOR THE ANNATTO OIL: Place the annatto seeds and oil in a pan over high heat. Cook until the oil turns a deep red color, 5 to 8 minutes. Set aside to cool.

FOR THE RAGOUT: Place the garlic and salt in a mortar and crush the garlic to a pulp. Add the lime juice, mix well and smear the mixture on the fish steaks. Set aside for 20 minutes. Grease a heatproof earthenware pot or casserole large enough to hold all the fish in a single layer. Arrange the fish steaks in the casserole and cover with the onion, tomato, green onion, and cilantro. Add 2 tablespoons of olive oil and 3 tablespoons of annatto oil.

Place the pot over high heat and bring to a boil. Lower the heat and cover the pot. Simmer for 10 minutes or until the fish is tender, adding water if it becomes to dry.

Serve in the pot with white rice, manioc meal, and pepper sauce.

Fish *with* Green Bananas

Peixe com Banana Verde

6 TO 8 SERVINGS

THIS FISH DISH IS TYPICAL of the northern coastal region of the State of São Paulo, and a portion of the southern coast of Rio de Janeiro. This dish is also known as *azul-marinho* (aquamarine sea) due to the coloring given by the green bananas.

3 POUNDS FISH STEAKS (GROUPER, SEA BASS, OR RED SNAPPER)	2 ONIONS, THINLY SLICED
SALT	3 CLOVES GARLIC, CRUSHED
2 TABLESPOONS LIME OR LEMON JUICE	3 LARGE TOMATOES, CHOPPED
¼ CUP CHOPPED FRESH CILANTRO	6 VERY GREEN BANANAS, UNPEELED AND HALVED LENGTHWISE
3 TABLESPOONS VEGETABLE OR OLIVE OIL	

Wash the fish steaks and place them in a deep dish. Sprinkle with salt and season with the lime juice and half of the cilantro. Heat the oil in a large pot that can also be used for serving (preferably earthenware) over medium heat. Add the onion and garlic and sauté until the onion is golden. Add the tomatoes and cook until soft. Add the bananas and 4 cups water and cook until the bananas are soft. Add the fish steaks in the casserole, cover, and allow to cook for about 10 minutes or until tender. Sprinkle with the remaining cilantro, taste for salt and serve immediately.

Holy Week Torte

Torta de Semana Santa

8 TO 10 SERVINGS

IN VITORIA, THE CAPITAL OF THE STATE OF ESPIRITO SANTO, many people continue to observe Easter as they did hundreds of years ago by serving this delicious dish during Holy Week. It is also customary to offer this torte to friends and neighbors as a token of good fellowship during the holiday. This torte was traditionally only eaten for supper on Good Friday, but today it is served at lunch as well and for supper on Holy Saturday and Easter Sunday. It is traditionally prepared in an earthenware casserole and can be served hot or cold.

TORTE:	1 POUND FRESH OYSTERS, IN THEIR
1 POUND SALT COD	JUICE
3 GARLIC CLOVES, MINCED	1 DOZEN FRESH CLAMS, SHUCKED
2 TEASPOONS SALT	1 POUND CRABMEAT
½ CUP VEGETABLE OIL	¼ CUP LEMON JUICE
2 LARGE ONIONS, MINCED	6 PALM HEARTS
1 JALAPEÑO PEPPER, MINCED	½ TEASPOON BLACK PEPPER
4 LARGE TOMATOES, PEELED AND	12 EGGS
CHOPPED	1 LARGE ONION, THINLY SLICED
¼ CUP FRESH PARSLEY	4 EGGS, HARD-BOILED AND SLICED
¼ CUP FRESH CILANTRO LEAVES	CROSSWISE
1 POUND LOBSTER MEAT	½ CUP SLICED BLACK OLIVES

Soak the salt cod in cold water for 24 hours, in the refrigerator, changing the water at least 4 times.

Pound the garlic and 1 teaspoon of the salt together in a mortar and pestle until they resemble a paste; set aside. Heat the vegetable oil in a large skillet and sauté the onions and jalapeño pepper until soft. Add the garlic paste, tomato, parsley, and cilantro, stirring to blend the vegetables together. Cover and simmer for 10 minutes.

Preheat the oven to 375°F and grease a 4-quart casserole. Reserving all the fish juices, add the salt cod, shrimp, lobster, oysters, clams, and crabmeat to the vegetables and simmer until the seafood is all cooked. Remove from the heat, stir in the lemon juice, cover, and let stand until cool, about 15 minutes.

Add the reserved juices, the palm hearts, and black pepper. Pour the mixture into the prepared casserole. Beat the eggs with the remaining 1 teaspoon of salt and pour over the mixture. Decorate the top with the onion slices, egg slices, and olives, placing the egg slices inside the onion slices and the olives around the onions.

Bake for 20 minutes or until a toothpick inserted in the center comes out clean. Cut into wedges and serve warm.

Seafood Torte

Torta Capixaba
10 SERVINGS

TORTA CAPIXABA IS THE STATE OF ESPIRITO SANTO'S best known dish. It dates back to the nineteenth century and was served during the meat-free days of Easter week. Today it is served throughout the year, but especially on Easter Sunday. The most popular fish for this dish are sea bass, grouper, and salt cod. The shellfish used are mussels, clams, oysters, crab, and shrimp.

3 TABLESPOONS OLIVE OIL	SALT
3 GARLIC CLOVES, CRUSHED	1 POUND FRESH SHRIMP, SHELLED AND
1 LARGE ONION, MINCED	DEVEINED
4 TOMATOES, SEEDED AND CHOPPED	1 POUND SALT COD, DESALTED AND
½ CUP CHOPPED GREEN ONIONS	SCALDED
1 TABLESPOON CHOPPED FRESH	2 CUPS COCONUT MILK
CILANTRO	1 CUP FRESHLY GRATED OR FRESH
1 RED BELL PEPPER, SEEDED AND	FROZEN UNSWEETENED COCONUT
CHOPPED	½ TEASPOON GROUND CLOVES
1 TABLESPOON ANNATTO OIL	½ TEASPOON GROUND CINNAMON
(PAGE 104) OR 1½ TEASPOONS	2 TABLESPOONS WHITE VINEGAR
EACH SAFFRON AND PAPRIKA	1 (7¾-OUNCE) CAN PALM HEARTS,
1 POUND FISH STEAKS (SEA BASS,	CHOPPED
GROUPER, HAKE)	½ CUP CHOPPED GREEN OLIVES
1 POUND MUSSELS AND/OR CLAMS,	4 EGGS, SCRAMBLED
SHELLED	6 EGGS, LIGHTLY BEATEN
1 POUND LUMP CRABMEAT	TOMATO SLICES FOR GARNISH
½ POUND SHELLED OYSTERS,	ONION SLICES FOR GARNISH
POACHED	

Preheat the oven to 350°F. Grease a 4-quart ovenproof casserole with olive oil.

Heat the olive oil in a large skillet and add the garlic and onion and sauté, stirring constantly until golden brown. Stir in the tomatoes, green onions, cilantro, red pepper, and annatto oil. Add the fish steaks, mussels, crabmeat, and oysters, stir and add salt to taste. Cover the skillet and simmer for 5 minutes. Add the shrimp and salt cod and cook for 2 minutes longer.

Remove the pan from the heat and cool uncovered for five minutes. Remove the fish steaks and salt cod from the pan and remove any bones. Flake the fish and salt cod into large pieces and return to the skillet. Add the coconut milk, grated coconut, cloves, cinnamon, vinegar, hearts of palm, and olives. Stir carefully and simmer uncovered until the liquid has almost evaporated. Mix in the scrambled eggs and pour the mixture into the prepared casserole. Pour the beaten eggs over the seafood mixture. Bake the torte for 10 minutes or until the eggs are almost set. Remove the casserole from the oven and decorate with slices of tomato and onion. Return to the oven and bake until golden.

Serve warm.

São Paulo-Style Shrimp Couscous

Cuscuz de Camarão à Paulista

6 SERVINGS

OF NORTH AFRICAN ORIGIN, couscous has traveled around the world. It was brought to Portugal by the Moors and later traveled to Brazil via Africa. In the Brazilian northeast, the term couscous refers to a cake made with tapioca, rice, or corn, coconut, and sugar and steamed. In the south, in São Paulo, it is popularly known as *Cuscuz Paulista*. The principal ingredient is cornmeal to which highly-seasoned fish, meat or poultry, and vegetables are added. The African version uses lamb and the meal is not mixed with the meat but cooked separately. The dish is a legacy of the Indians, who lent it the cornmeal, and the backland pioneers with their food wrapped in cloth sacks to eat on the trail.

Today couscous has a sophisticated appearance, but retains its rustic and delicious 500-year-old character. Couscous is usually served at parties and special occasions. The preparation may seem very time-consuming, and the ingredients many, but your patience will be rewarded with a gastronomic delight.

COUSCOUS:
4 CUPS WHITE CORNMEAL
1 TABLESPOON MANIOC FLOUR
1 TEASPOON SALT
½ CUP BUTTER

SHRIMP:
½ POUND LARGE SHRIMP
1 POUND MEDIUM-SIZE SHRIMP
2 TABLESPOONS LEMON JUICE
1 TEASPOON SALT
½ TEASPOON BLACK PEPPER
½ CUP BUTTER OR VEGETABLE OIL
⅓ CUP GRATED ONION
2 TABLESPOONS CHOPPED FRESH
  PARSLEY

1 CUP CANNED TOMATO SAUCE
1 TEASPOON RED PEPPER FLAKES

ASSEMBLY:
3 TOMATOES, PEELED AND CHOPPED
3 EGGS, HARD-BOILED AND SLICED
½ CUP PITTED BLACK OLIVES
1 (4-OUNCE) CAN SARDINES IN
  TOMATO SAUCE
2 HEARTS OF PALM, CUT INTO
  ½-INCH SLICES
1 GREEN BELL PEPPER, SEEDED AND
  SLICED
1 LARGE COLLARD GREEN LEAF OR A
  WHITE CLOTH NAPKIN

Preheat the oven to 350°F.

FOR THE COUSCOUS: Mix together the cornmeal and manioc flour and place in a baking dish. Bake for 5 minutes, stirring once a minute so that it toasts evenly. Bring 1 cup water to a boil with the salt. Sprinkle the cornmeal mixture with the boiling water. Mix well with a fork and return to the oven for another 2 minutes. The mixture will be a little lumpy. Add the butter and mix well.

FOR THE SHRIMP: Peel, devein, rinse, and dry the shrimp. Place in a large bowl and add the lemon juice, salt, and pepper. Marinate for 1 hour. Melt the butter in a large skillet; add the onion and the parsley. Sauté the onions for 3 minutes. Add the shrimp and cook 2 minutes. Add the tomato sauce and the red pepper flakes, cover, reduce the heat to a simmer, and cook until the shrimp are pink. Remove the large shrimp and reserve for decorating the couscous. Add the cornmeal mixture to the remaining shrimp and mix well.

FOR THE ASSEMBLY: In a couscous steamer or a colander decoratively arrange the tomatoes, eggs, olives, and sardine halves on the bottom and sides of the pan, and top with ¼ of the couscous mixture, the hearts of palm, and peppers. Press the large shrimp and the sardines into the couscous on the sides of the pan in a decorative pattern. Continue to form layers with the ingredients until all are used. Cover the pan with the collard green leaf or the napkin and cook over boiling water until the collard green leaf is cooked or the napkin is completely wet and the mixture is cooked and dry (about 30 minutes). Let cool for 10 minutes and turn out onto a serving platter.

NOTE: The original recipe calls for corn flour, which can be found is Latin American, Mexican, Asian, and specialty markets. I have used finely ground cornmeal which is a good substitute.

Shrimp *with* Chayote

Camarão Ensopado com Chuchu

6 SERVINGS

THE NAME OF THIS RECIPE is apparently the title of a song. Carmen Miranda (1909-1955), the famous singer and movie star, who although born in Portugal (her parents took her to Rio when she was two years old) became a performer often referred to as "The Brazilian Bombshell." She was well known for her exotic hats piled high with bananas and other tropical fruits. In the 1940s she gained popularity in the U.S., where she performed in night clubs and acted in films. When she returned to Rio de Janeiro, after a prolonged stay in the U.S., she was accused of having become Americanized. During a public appearance in Rio, in order to affirm her Brazilian identity she gave a rendition of *Camarão Ensopado com Chuchu*, the first verse of which translate as: "When you hear the tambourines playing when it's time to eat, you can be sure that I will choose a shrimp stew with chayote." In Rio you can enjoy this dish at one of her favorite restaurants, The Penafiel, which has been in existence since 1913. Or you can prepare it at home for friends who may remember Carmen Miranda.

1½ POUNDS SMALL SHRIMP, SHELLED, DEVEINED, RINSED, AND DRAINED
2 TABLESPOONS LEMON OR LIME JUICE
SALT AND BLACK PEPPER
2 TABLESPOONS CHOPPED FRESH CILANTRO OR PARSLEY
¼ CUP OLIVE OIL

1 MEDIUM-SIZE ONION, CHOPPED
2 CLOVES GARLIC, CHOPPED
3 LARGE TOMATOES, PEELED, SEEDED, AND CHOPPED
2 MEDIUM-SIZE CHAYOTES, PEELED AND CUBED

In a nonreactive bowl, combine the shrimp, lemon juice, salt and black pepper, and half of the cilantro. Set aside for 10 minutes.

Heat the oil in a skillet over high heat and add the onions and garlic and sauté until the onion is golden. Add the shrimp and cook until pink. Add the tomato and chayote, cover and reduce the heat. Cook, stirring occasionally for about 15 minutes or until the chayote is soft. Remove from the heat and sprinkle with the remaining cilantro.

Arrange on a platter and serve with white rice and hot pepper sauce.

Minas Gerais-Style Greens

Couve à Mineira
8 TO 10 SERVINGS

GREENS, ALONG WITH BEANS AND CORN MUSH, make up the traditional Minas trio of foods. The greens are usually *couve galega*, a type of cabbage grown in Portugal that is similar to collard greens. The Portuguese took these greens to Brazil, Angola, Cape Verde, and Guinea-Bissau.

These greens usually accompany the Brazilian national dish *Feijoada* (page 54) as well as *Tutu à Mineira* (page 116), and *Feijão Tropeira* (page 114).

5 TABLESPOONS OLIVE OIL	½ TEASPOON BLACK PEPPER
3 LARGE BUNCHES COLLARD GREENS	1 TEASPOON CRUSHED RED PEPPER
1 MEDIUM ONION, FINELY CHOPPED	FLAKES
2 LARGE GARLIC CLOVES, MINCED	
1 TEASPOON SALT	

Bring a large pot of water with 2 tablespoons of the olive oil to a boil. Remove the ribs from the collard greens. Stack the leaves one on top of the other and then roll up tightly like a cigar. Slice each roll into ⅛-inch slices or thinner if possible. Blanch the greens in the boiling water for 5 minutes then drain and set aside. Heat the remaining 3 tablespoons of olive oil in a large skillet. Sauté the onions and garlic until the onions are translucent then season with salt and black pepper. Add the greens and red pepper flakes and sauté for 3 minutes, stirring constantly so that the greens do not loose their bright green color. Serve hot.

Trooper Beans

Feijão Tropeiro

10 SERVINGS

TRAVELERS ON THE ROADS OF MINAS GERAIS usually had four types of accommodations to choose from: the *pouso* or resting place, an area where farmers would let horseback riders camp to prepare lunch or pass the night in the open. After obtaining the owners' permission, the rider would water the animals, prepare his dinner and then bed down for the night atop saddlebags and harnesses. Other accommodations were the *rancho*, a simple hut, the *venda*, the back room of a small grocery store, and the *estalagem*, an inn. The *pouso* was the preference of most travelers. Those who traveled in caravans usually traveled with a cook who would prepare a meal of beans mixed with dried beef and serve it with the usual cup of coffee. That night the cook would prepare another pot of beans and let it simmer all night to be ready for the next day. Dried beans and dried beef were the two foods that could withstand the long journey and not spoil.

The old trooper lent his name to this traditional dish, trooper beans. The name is a token of homage to the brave men who carried supplies and helped tame the hinterlands.

Today *feijão tropeiro* is daily fare for families from Minas and the dish has been enhanced with corn purée, pork cracklings, shredded collard greens, and manioc flour, an Indian contribution. This dish is also called *feijão-das-onze*—eleven o'clock beans because it is usually served for lunch, and *feijão-de-preguiça*—lazy beans.

2 POUNDS DRY BLACK BEANS (4½ CUPS)	1 CUP MANIOC FLOUR
2 POUNDS BACON FAT	2 EGGS, HARD-BOILED
SALT	2 TABLESPOONS CHOPPED GREEN
2 POUNDS PORK SAUSAGE	ONIONS
2 GARLIC CLOVES, SMASHED	
3 SMALL ONIONS, THINLY SLICED	

Rinse the beans and soak over night in cold water to cover. The following day, drain the beans, place in a pot of cold water over high heat and bring to a boil. Reduce the heat, cover and simmer for 2 hours. Drain the beans reserving the cooking liquid. Cut the bacon fat into ½–inch pieces. Heat a skillet and fry the bacon pieces with the salt until golden. Remove the bacon and reserve the fat. In another skillet, place the sausage and 1 cup of water. Cover the pan and cook the sausage until the water evaporates. Uncover and brown on all sides. Remove and reserve. Heat ½ cup of the reserved bacon grease and sauté the garlic, onions, and strained beans. Add the manioc flour, cracklings, and green onions.

TO SERVE: Place the bean mixture in the center of a large serving platter. Decorate the edges with slices of sausage and hard-boiled eggs. Serve with shredded collard greens, white rice, and golden fried onions.

Bean Purée *with* Sausages

Tutu à Mineira

10 SERVINGS

BEANS ARE THE MAINSTAY of Mineira cuisine particularly the brown bean, known as *mulatinho*. The dish that is most characteristic of this cuisine is *tutu de feijão* or *tutu à Mineira*. The word tutu is a corruption of *quitutu*, a word from Kimbundu, a Bantu language of Angola, which curiously enough means *papa*, a supernatural creature. One might surmise that this dish is so tasty that it appears to have come from another world. The puréed beans are thickened with manioc flour and served with pork cracklings, pork sausage, hard-boiled eggs and shredded collard greens. It is truly an other worldly feast.

BEANS:	SAUSAGES:
2 CUPS DRY KIDNEY BEANS	3 POUNDS FRESH PORK SAUSAGE
3 TABLESPOONS VEGETABLE OIL OR BACON GREASE	2 TABLESPOONS VEGETABLE OIL OR BACON GREASE
1 LARGE ONION, MINCED	
2 GARLIC CLOVES, SMASHED	GARNISH:
1 CUP MANIOC FLOUR	2 TABLESPOONS OIL OR BACON GREASE
¼ CUP CHOPPED FRESH PARSLEY	1 TABLESPOON WHITE VINEGAR
¼ CUP CHOPPED GREEN ONIONS	2 LARGE ONIONS, SLICED
1 TEASPOON SALT	1 TEASPOON SALT
1 TO 2 SMALL GREEN BELL PEPPERS, SEEDED AND CHOPPED	5 EGGS, HARD-BOILED AND SLICED

FOR THE BEANS: Pick over the beans, then rinse and soak them in cold water to cover for 4 hours or overnight. Drain the beans and place them in a large pot with cold water to cover plus 5 inches and cook over high heat. When the beans begin to boil, cover, reduce the heat and simmer until tender, about 2 hours. Place the beans and 1 cup of the cooking liquid in a food processor or blender and purée, add more water if necessary. Set aside.

Heat the oil in a large skillet over high heat. Add the onion and garlic and brown slightly. Add the bean purée and bring to a boil. Sprinkle the beans with the manioc flour, mix well and cook, stirring until the mixture thickens. Add the parsley, green onions, salt, and green pepper. Remove from the heat and set aside.

FOR THE SAUSAGE: In a large skillet, combine the sausages, oil, and 2 cups water over high heat and cook until the water evaporates. Let the sausages fry in their own oil, turning to brown on all sides. If the sausages begin to stick, add a little more oil. Remove from the pan and drain on absorbent paper. Cut into 1-inch slices and set aside.

FOR THE GARNISH: Heat the oil in a pan over medium high heat. Add the vinegar and the onions and cook until tender. Add salt to taste and set aside.

TO SERVE: Place half the bean mixture on half of a large platter and cover with half of the hard-boiled eggs, sausage, and the onions. Cover with the rest of the bean mixture, decorate with egg slices, sausage, and the remaining onions. Serve with a roasted pork loin, Mineira-Style Greens (page 113), rice, and pork cracklings.

Brazilian-Style Succotash

Pudim de Milho e Feijão

8 SERVINGS

IN THE SIXTEENTH AND SEVENTEENTH CENTURIES, because of religious and dietary restrictions, many Jewish immigrants chose this dish, when dining with their Christian friends. Because this succotash was a popular dish with the entire Brazilian population, when the secret Jews ate with their Catholic friends, they could profess a preference for this dish over dishes containing pork and thus were able to honor their religious dietary restrictions and avoid eating prohibited foods without drawing attention to their religion.

1 (10-OUNCE) PACKAGE FROZEN LIMA BEANS	1 TABLESPOON SUGAR
1 (10-OUNCE) PACKAGE FROZEN CORN	¼ TEASPOON GROUND NUTMEG
3 EGGS, LIGHTLY BEATEN	¼ CUP BUTTER
3 TABLESPOONS FLOUR	1 SMALL ONION, MINCED
1 TEASPOON BLACK PEPPER	½ GREEN BELL PEPPER, MINCED
	2 CUPS HALF-AND-HALF

Preheat the oven to 325°F. Grease a 2-quart ovenproof casserole. Combine the lima beans, corn, and eggs in a medium-sized bowl. In another bowl combine the flour, salt, pepper, sugar, and nutmeg. Heat the butter in a medium pot and sauté the onion and green pepper until soft. Add the flour mixture to the onion mixture and stir well. Stir in the half-and-half and add the vegetable mixture. Pour into the prepared casserole. Place the casserole in a larger pan with hot water to a depth of 1 inch, to form a bain-marie. Bake for 1 hour or until a toothpick inserted comes out clean. Serve warm with roast pork or beef.

Rice Salad

Salada de Arroz

4 SERVINGS

RICE SALADS ARE AS POPULAR IN BRAZIL, as they are in the rest of the Portuguese-speaking world. Each country or territory uses slightly different ingredients. In Brazil, the most popular ingredients are canned peas, apple, and avocado with beets, shrimp, or hard-boiled eggs for garnish. This particular salad can be made with white or Brazilian rice.

SALAD:	2 TABLESPOONS OLIVE OIL
2 CUPS COLD COOKED RICE	1 TEASPOON MUSTARD
1 TART GREEN APPLE, CORED, PEELED	1 TEASPOON SALT
AND JULIENNED	¼ TEASPOON BLACK PEPPER
½ AVOCADO, PEELED AND SLICED	
1 TABLESPOON CHOPPED PIMIENTO	GARNISH:
1 CUP CANNED OR FROZEN PEAS,	½ HEAD LETTUCE, SHREDDED
COOKED	3 HARD BOILED EGGS
1 TABLESPOON LEMON JUICE	½ POUND SHRIMP, COOKED, PEELED,
1 TABLESPOON WHITE VINEGAR	AND DEVEINED

Place the rice in a large bowl. Add the apple, avocado, pimiento, and peas. In a smaller bowl, mix the lemon juice, vinegar, olive oil, mustard, salt, and pepper. Add this dressing to the rice and vegetables, mix well and pack into a 1-quart mold. Chill for at least 2 hours.

Arrange the lettuce on a platter and turn out the rice on top. Decorate the platter with sliced hard-boiled eggs and shrimp.

Mountain Rice

Arroz da Serra

6 TO 8 SERVINGS

THIS RICE DISH COMES FROM THE *SERTÃO* or "backlands" of the southern Brazilian state of São Paulo. The inhabitants of this region are called *Caipiras*, a term roughly equivalent to "yokel" or "hayseed." Actually, the word is a Portuguese corruption of *caapora*, which in the language of the Tupi-Guarani means "forest dwellers." Dating back to the sixteenth century these backlanders lived among the Indians, from whom they adopted many cultural and social ways, including food customs.

This is one of the dishes influenced by the Tupi-Guarani that is now a part of Brazil's cuisine.

2 CUPS WHITE RICE	6 GREEN BANANAS, PEELED AND CUT
1 TABLESPOON VEGETABLE OIL	INTO ½-INCH SLICES
1 POUND GROUND BEEF	8 OUNCES FRESH GOAT CHEESE

Preheat the oven to 350°F and grease a 2-quart ovenproof casserole.

Bring 4 cups of water to a boil. Stir in the rice, cover, reduce the heat and simmer for 20 minutes. Meanwhile, sauté the beef in a skillet until browned. Set aside.

Heat the oil in a large skillet and brown the bananas quickly on each side. Remove and drain on absorbent paper.

Layer the ingredients in the casserole. Begin with half the rice, then half the ground beef, cheese, and banana. Top with a second layer of the ingredients, ending with bananas. Bake the casserole for 15 minutes or until the cheese is melted.

Serve warm.

Stuffed Bread *with* Ham *and* Cheese

Pão Enrolado
MAKES 1 LOAF

WHILE VISITING MY OLD FRIENDS Antonio and Isabel Buitos Carelli in São Paulo, their daughter, Fabiana, prepared this wonderful stuffed bread for us. It is a favorite of many *Paulistas* and like pizza, the recipe originated in the Italian community.

3 TABLESPOONS BAKING POWDER OR 3 CUBES FRESH YEAST	8 OUNCES HAM OR SMOKED SAUSAGE, THINLY SLICED
1 CUP WARM MILK	2 MEDIUM TOMATOES, THINLY SLICED
2 CUPS FLOUR	2 CUPS GRATED MOZZARELLA CHEESE (8 OUNCES)
½ CUP VEGETABLE OIL	¼ CUP CHOPPED FRESH OREGANO
2 TEASPOONS SUGAR	
1 TEASPOON SALT	

Dissolve the baking powder in the warm milk. Place the flour in a large bowl and add the oil, sugar, salt, and baking powder mixture. Stir the ingredients until a dough forms. Roll out the dough to form a 9 x 11-inch rectangle. Arrange a layer of ham on top of the dough. Place the tomato slices on top of the meat. Sprinkle the tomatoes with the grated cheese and the oregano. Roll up the dough beginning with one of the long sides. Place on the prepared baking sheet and let rise in a warm place for 60 minutes.

Preheat the oven to 400°F and grease a baking sheet. Bake for 30 minutes or until golden.

Serve warm cut into 1-inch slices.

Minas Cheese Rolls

Pãezinhos de Queijo

MAKES 2 DOZEN ROLLS

MINAS GERAIS IS KNOWN for these little cheese rolls made with goat cheese. They are popular as a snack or served with meals. You can substitute Parmesan for the goat cheese without altering the taste.

1 CUP WHOLE MILK	4 CUPS MANIOC FLOUR
½ CUP BUTTER, MELTED	5 EGGS
1 TABLESPOON SALT	2 CUPS GRATED FRESH GOAT CHEESE

Heat the oven to 375°F and lightly grease a baking sheet.

Heat 1 cup of water, the milk, butter, and salt in a pan over medium heat until hot, but not boiling. Place the flour in a large bowl and pour in the hot liquid. Mix well and allow to cool. Add the eggs one at a time and lastly the cheese. Mix well. Form the dough into balls the size of walnuts. Place on the prepared baking sheet. Make a slit on top of each roll with a sharp knife. Bake for about 20 minutes, or until lightly golden.

Serve warm.

Manioc *and* Peanut Meal

Paçoca de Amendoim

6 TO 8 SERVINGS

DURING HOLY WEEK *Paçoca* is served in many homes in the valley of the Paraíba River. Whole fresh bananas always accompany this dessert.

4 CUPS UNSALTED PEANUTS, WITHOUT SKINS, TOASTED (1½ POUNDS)	3 CUPS SUGAR
4 CUPS MANIOC FLOUR, TOASTED	½ TEASPOON SALT

Place the peanuts, 1 cup at a time, in a food processor or blender and process until they resemble a fine meal. Place in a bowl with the manioc flour and the sugar. Mix well. Sift the mixture through a strainer to assure that it is uniform. Place in a bowl and serve with peeled, ripe bananas.

NOTE: This will keep for a week in a covered container.

Half-Moon Cookies

Biscoitos Meia-Lua

MAKES 30 COOKIES

THE RECIPE FOR THESE COOKIES, shaped like half-moons, has been passed down from generation to generation by families in Minas Gerais. They are usually served as a snack with afternoon coffee or as a dessert after dinner. These cookies are also known as *quitandas*, which means finger foods.

3 CUPS FLOUR	1 CUP PEANUTS, TOASTED AND
1½ CUPS SUGAR	GROUND (4 OUNCES)
1½ CUPS BUTTER	½ CUP SUGAR
2 EGG YOLKS, LIGHTLY BEATEN	

Preheat the oven to 350°F. Grease and flour a baking sheet.

Combine the flour and sugar and cut the butter into the mixture, ½ cup at a time. Knead until a dough forms that can be rolled out with a rolling pin. Place half the dough between two sheets of plastic wrap and roll out ¼ inch thick. Remove the top sheet of plastic and cut the cookies into half moons. Arrange the cookies on the prepared baking sheet. Repeat until all the dough is used. Brush the cookies with egg yolk and sprinkle with the peanuts.

Bake for 12 minutes, or until lightly golden. Remove from the oven and sprinkle with sugar. Place on racks to cool.

Chocolate Bonbons

Brigadeiros

MAKES ABOUT 20 BALLS

THESE CHOCOLATES WERE NAMED for Brigadier General Eduardo Gomes, a famous Brazilian Air Force commander from the 1940s, who was a chocoholic. A local restaurant in São Paulo developed the recipe for him and they have since become a favorite at parties and other festive occasions throughout Brazil.

1 (14-OUNCE) CAN SWEETENED CONDENSED MILK	1 TABLESPOON BUTTER
¼ CUP UNSWEETENED COCOA	¼ TEASPOON SALT
	1 CUP CHOCOLATE SPRINKLES

In a medium-size pan, combine the sweetened condensed milk and cocoa powder. Cook over low heat, stirring constantly with a wooden spoon until the mixture pulls away from the sides of the pan, about 20 minutes. Add the butter and salt and mix thoroughly before removing the mixture from the heat. When the mixture is cool, grease your hands with butter and shape into 1-inch balls. Roll in chocolate sprinkles and place in miniature silver or paper cupcake liners. Store the balls in the refrigerator until ready to serve.

Manioc Pudding

Pudim de Mandioca

8 SERVINGS

THIS RECIPE HAS BEEN POPULAR in São Paulo for the past century and its popularity has spread to all parts of Brazil. In the northeast it is prepared without the caramel coating, which I believe adds a special touch.

½ CUP SUGAR	1 CUP WHOLE MILK
2 CUPS FINELY GRATED MANIOC ROOT (SEE NOTE)	6 EGGS, LIGHTLY BEATEN
	3 TABLESPOONS BUTTER, MELTED AND
1 CUP FINELY GRATED FRESH OR	COOLED
FROZEN UNSWEETENED COCONUT	1 TABLESPOON FLOUR
2½ CUPS SUGAR	

Preheat the oven to 350°F.

Combine the sugar and ½ cup water in a small saucepan over high heat, stirring constantly just until the sugar is dissolved. Stop stirring and let the mixture boil until it turns light golden brown. Remove from the heat and pour into a tube pan turning so that the syrup coats the bottom and sides of the pan. Set aside.

Place the grated manioc root, coconut, sugar, milk, eggs, melted butter, and flour in a large bowl and mix well. Pour the mixture into the pan. Set the pan in a larger baking pan filled with ½ inch of hot water forming a bain-marie. Bake for 40 minutes or until golden brown. Remove from the oven and let it cool on a rack. Chill the pudding in the pan in the refrigerator for at least 4 hours. Turn out onto a serving dish just before serving.

NOTE: To grate the manioc, peel a (1-pound) manioc root and cut in half widthwise and lengthwise. Remove the center core and grate the remaining pieces on the small-hole side of a cheese grater.

Rum Drink

Batida Paulista

2 SERVINGS

THE LITERAL TRANSLATION OF *BATIDA* is "beaten" but, this drink is actually shaken. It is a slightly tart drink made with *cachaça*, a rum made from sugarcane instead of molasses. Many would say that a bean stew (*Feijoada Baiana*, page 54) is not complete without a *batida*.

4 OUNCES *CACHAÇA* OR WHITE RUM	1 EGG WHITE, LIGHTLY BEATEN AND
2 TABLESPOONS LEMON JUICE	STRAINED
2 TEASPOONS SUGAR PLUS	¼ CUP ICE CUBES, CRUSHED
ADDITIONAL FOR GARNISH	

Shake all the ingredients in a cocktail shaker. Moisten the rim of the glasses with a damp cloth and then dip in sugar. Pour into glasses and serve immediately.

VARIATIONS:

COFFEE BATIDA: 1 jigger *cachaça* (or white rum), 1 teaspoon sugar, ¼ cup strong cold coffee, 1 egg white lightly beaten and strained, and cracked ice. Shake well.

PINEAPPLE BATIDA: 1jigger pineapple juice, 1 teaspoon sugar, 4 teaspoons lemon juice, 2 jiggers white rum or *cachaça*, and cracked ice. Shake well.

COCONUT MILK BATIDA: 1 cup coconut milk, 1 cup milk, ½ cup gin, ½ cup *cachaça* (or white rum), and sugar to taste. Shake well; add 1 crushed ice cube and chill before serving. (Serves 6)

Center West Cuisine

The center west region consists of the states of Mato Grosso, Mato Grosso do Sul and Goiás where the Federal District and the country's capital, Brasilia is located. Mato Grosso borders Bolivia and Paraguay, and its cuisine is influenced by these two neighboring countries. Mato Grosso do Sul is also bordered by the state of Paraná to the south and its gaucho (cowboy) cuisine, which is based mainly on grilled meats, has influenced the state's cuisine as well.

The Black River, which runs through Mato Grosso, provides plenty of fish, including the dreaded piranha. Many people live along the banks of the river and consume their daily catch. A typical meal in the Pantanal region includes fish, prepared in one of many different ways, grilled, fried, dried, in soups, and dried cooked with vegetables. Besides fish and grilled beef, Mato Grosso is known for its fruit, such as the *mangaba*, *guarioba*, *pitanga*, *maxixe*, and *pequi*. Because the state is so large, many of these fruits are regional and only known where they are grown.

Alligator is another popular food of the inhabitants of this region. It has a taste similar to that of fish and the tail meat is often used as a filling for fried manioc balls. Another popular dish is *camambuco*, a fried patty made of alligator, and mashed potatoes or manioc. They also enjoy a dish of dried beef with manioc (*caribéu*) which is great on a cold winter's night.

In the state of Goiás, the cuisine is similar to that of Minas Gerais. We find an *empadão* filled with chicken and cheese, *pastelinho* and a miniature caramel tart of Portuguese influence that is similar to the Belem tart. Corn is also an important ingredient in the diet. Dishes like *pamonha*, creamed corn cooked in corn husks and boiled is very popular at parties.

Corn Omelet

Omelete de Milho

4 SERVINGS

CORN, WHICH IS GROWN in the central-west region is a staple in the region's diet. There are many corn dishes that the local population enjoys such as *Pamonha* (page 136). This recipe for a fresh corn omelet topped with Parmesan cheese is a bit unusual but very tasty.

6 EARS OF CORN, HUSKED OR 1 (10-OUNCE) CAN CORN, DRAINED	2 TABLESPOONS CHOPPED FRESH PARSLEY
6 EGGS	2 TABLESPOONS CHOPPED GREEN ONION
1 TEASPOON SALT	¼ CUP PARMESAN CHEESE
1 TABLESPOON VEGETABLE OIL	
1 MEDIUM ONION, MINCED	

Place the ears of corn in a glass dish with 3 tablespoons of water and microwave on high for 5 minutes. With a sharp knife cut the kernels from the cob and place in a blender with the eggs and salt. Beat until smooth. Heat the oil in a skillet, over medium heat, and pour the egg mixture into the skillet. Sprinkle the onion over the egg, cover, and cook for 3 minutes or until top is firm. Using a large spatula fold omelet in half, remove and place on a platter. Sprinkle with the parsley, green onions, and Parmesan cheese. Serve immediately.

Baked Chicken Turnovers

Saltenhas
MAKES 20 PASTRIES

THIS BAKED PASTRY is very similar to Argentine's beef empanada. The Mato Grosso version uses chicken instead of beef and annatto coloring to give the dough a slightly reddish color. If annatto coloring is not available, substitute saffron or paprika.

DOUGH:	2 TABLESPOONS LARD OR SHORTENING
1½ CUPS LARD OR SHORTENING	1 LARGE ONION, FINELY CHOPPED
1 TABLESPOON ANNATTO SEEDS	2 GARLIC CLOVES, CRUSHED
1 TABLESPOON SALT	2 POUNDS CHICKEN, COOKED AND
7½ CUPS FLOUR	SHREDDED
	3 MEDIUM YUKON GOLD POTATOES
FILLING:	COOKED, PEELED, AND DICED
2 TABLESPOONS PLUS 1 TEASPOON	1 CUP RAISINS
ANNATTO COLORING (SEE NOTE)	1 CUP SMALL PITTED BLACK OLIVES
¼ CUP FLOUR	1 CUP CANNED PEAS, DRAINED
SALT AND BLACK PEPPER	2 EGGS, HARD-BOILED AND CHOPPED
½ TEASPOON CUMIN	2 EGG YOLKS, LIGHTLY BEATEN
1 TEASPOON OREGANO	

FOR THE DOUGH: Heat the annatto seeds with the lard, stirring until the lard melts. Strain, add 1½ cups water and salt and let cool to lukewarm. Gradually add the flour, kneading until the dough is elastic and no longer sticks to your hands. Place in a greased bowl, cover with plastic and let sit for 30 minutes.

FOR THE FILLING: In a small pan mix the annatto coloring with the flour and 1½ cups water. Cook until thick and smooth, stirring constantly. Season with salt, pepper, cumin, and oregano, remove from the heat and set aside.

Place the lard in a large pan with 1 teaspoon of the annatto coloring, the onion and garlic. Sauté, stirring constantly to prevent the mixture from sticking. Add the chicken, mix well and simmer for 5 minutes. Remove from the heat and add the potatoes. Let cool, then stir in the raisins, olives, peas, and chopped eggs.

Preheat the oven to 350°F. Lightly dust 2 baking sheets with flour. Divide the dough into 20 balls. Roll each ball into an 8-inch circle, on a floured surface.

Place ½ cup of the filling in the center of each circle. Fold in half and seal the edges by twisting them together with your thumb and forefinger. Brush lightly with the egg yolk. Place the pastries standing up so that the pinched edge is on the top. Bake for about 30 minutes or until golden. Serve hot with a green salad.

NOTE: Annatto coloring is made by melting lard or shortening with annatto seeds and then straining the mixture. The preferred fat for these pastries is lard, but shortening is a good substitute.

Goiás Meat *and* Cheese Pies

Empadão Goiano
MAKES 20 PIES

THESE LITTLE PIES are just the right size for an afternoon snack or as part of an appetizer buffet. They are also served as a light meal accompanied by a salad. These pies are one of the best known regional dishes and are identified with the state of Goiás. Leftover roast chicken, turkey and pork are ideal to use for this dish.

DOUGH:
8 CUPS FLOUR
1 TABLESPOON BAKING POWDER
1½ TEASPOONS SALT
2 CUPS BUTTER OR LARD, CUT INTO
  1-INCH PIECES
3 EGG YOLKS, LIGHTLY BEATEN

FILLING:
½ CUP LARD OR SHORTENING
6 POUNDS BONELESS, SKINLESS
  CHICKEN BREASTS
1 POUND BONELESS PORK LOIN
4 EGGS, HARD-BOILED AND DICED
1½ CUPS FARMER'S CHEESE, DICED

20 BLACK OLIVES, PITTED
1 (7¾-OUNCE) CAN PALM HEARTS,
  DRAINED AND DICED
½ CUP CHOPPED FRESH PARSLEY
½ CUP CHOPPED GREEN ONIONS

SAUCE:
2 (10-OUNCE) CANS TOMATO SAUCE
1 (6-OUNCE) CAN TOMATO PASTE
½ CUP CHOPPED FRESH PARSLEY
½ CUP CHOPPED GREEN ONIONS
A FEW DASHES HOT PEPPER SAUCE
1 TEASPOON BLACK PEPPER
¼ CUP FLOUR

FOR THE DOUGH: In a large bowl mix the flour and baking powder. Cut in the shortening with a pastry blender or 2 knives until the mixture resembles coarse meal. The texture will not be uniform but will contain crumbs and small bits and pieces. Stir the salt into 1 cup lukewarm water. Add the water and knead until a soft dough forms. Shape into a ball, cover with a cloth, and allow to rest for 1 hour.

FOR THE FILLING: Melt the lard in a large skillet and sauté the chicken breasts, covered, until cooked through, turning to brown lightly on all sides. Remove. Let cool and shred. In the same pan, brown the pork loin on all sides. Remove the pork, cool, and shred.

FOR THE SAUCE: Add the tomato sauce, tomato paste, parsley, green onions, pepper sauce, and pepper to the same pan in which the chicken and pork were fried. Dissolve the flour in ¼ cup cold water and stir until smooth. Add 8 cups of water and the flour mixture to the tomato sauce. Cook. stirring, over low heat until the sauce thickens slightly. Cool completely before filling the pies.

Preheat the oven to 350°F and set out 2 muffin tins or 20 individual tart pans. Roll out the dough ¼ inch thick. Cut out 20 (4-inch) and 20 (3-inch) circles and press the larger circles into the bottom and up the sides of the tins. Layer the filling in each tin in the following order: chicken, pork, eggs, cheese, 1 olive, and 1 teaspoon palm hearts. Top with 1 tablespoon of sauce and cover with a 3-inch circle of dough. Press around the edges to seal. Brush with the egg yolk and bake for about 20 minutes or until golden brown. Cool slightly and turn out onto a serving tray.

Serve at room temperature.

NOTE: If using tart tins, place them on a baking sheet and bake until golden brown.

Piranha Soup

Caldo de Piranha

10 SERVINGS

THE PIRANHA, terrifying to some because of tales of its carnivorous nature, is actually one of the most flavorful fresh water fish I've ever tasted. Although it is usually a small fish, some grow to two feet and weigh up to three pounds. People of the wetlands say that they will only attack when they are trapped.

Since piranhas are not allowed in the United States, you can substitute walleye or any other sweet, white, freshwater fish.

4 POUNDS SMALL FISH (ABOUT 6 OUNCES EACH), CLEANED AND CUT INTO 1-INCH PIECES	BOILING WATER
	2 LARGE TOMATOES, PEELED, SEEDED, AND CHOPPED
3 GARLIC CLOVES, CRUSHED	1 LARGE RED PEPPER, SEEDED AND
3 TABLESPOONS LIME OR LEMON JUICE	JULIENNED
1 TABLESPOON WHITE VINEGAR	1 MEDIUM ONION, CHOPPED
1 TEASPOON SALT	1 TABLESPOON CHOPPED GREEN
½ TEASPOON BLACK PEPPER	ONIONS
½ CUP PLUS 2 TABLESPOONS VEGETABLE OIL	2 TABLESPOONS CHOPPED FRESH CILANTRO

Place the fish pieces in a large bowl and season with the garlic, lime juice, vinegar, salt, and pepper. Marinate for at least 2 hours in the refrigerator.

Heat ½ cup of the oil in a large skillet over high heat. Add the fish and sauté for 3 minutes. Pour in enough boiling water to fill the skillet halfway, cover, reduce the heat to simmer and cook for 10 minutes. Remove from the heat, and strain, reserving the broth.

Remove the skin and any bones from the fish. Place the fish and the broth in a blender and process until creamy. Set aside. Heat 2 tablespoons of oil in a pan over high heat and add the tomatoes, bell pepper, and onion. Simmer until soft, add the fish mixture, green onions, and cilantro. Stir the mixture until hot.

Remove the pan from the heat, pour into a soup terrine, and serve with hot pepper sauce.

Mato Grosso-Style Pasta

Macarronada Pantaneira
4 SERVINGS

THE ITALIAN INFLUENCE on the indigenous is evident in this dish of pasta and dried beef. This dish is very popular and is served at lunch and dinner with a glass of red wine.

The dried beef has to soak over night, so begin preparation the day before serving.

1 POUND BRAZILIAN DRIED BEEF	2 GARLIC CLOVES, SMASHED
1 (1-POUND) PACKAGE CORKSCREW	½ TEASPOON BLACK PEPPER
PASTA	3 TABLESPOONS TOMATO PASTE
1 TEASPOON SALT	½ CUP CHOPPED FRESH PARSLEY
3 TABLESPOONS OLIVE OIL	½ CUP CHOPPED GREEN ONIONS
1 ONION, GRATED	

Soak the dried beef in water to cover overnight. The following day remove the beef from the water, trim any fat and cut into cubes. Place the beef in a pot with water to cover, bring to a boil and cook for 10 minutes. Drain and set aside.

Bring a large pot of water to a boil with the salt. Add the pasta and cook according to the package directions. Drain the pasta and keep warm.

Heat the oil in a skillet, add the beef, onion, garlic, pepper, tomato paste, parsley, and green onions. Add ½ cup water, cover, and cook over low heat for about 10 minutes. Keep and eye on the pan so that the mixture doesn't dry out. Add more water as necessary. Place the pasta in a serving bowl and pour the beef mixture over it. Mix well and serve with a green salad.

Creamed Corn *in* Husks

Pamonha

MAKES 30 PACKETS

PAMONHA IS A NATIVE Brazilian specialty. The word comes from the Tupi Guarani language and describes a type of corn cake that is wrapped in corn husks and boiled. These cakes are a favorite throughout Brazil, but are widely available in shops, restaurants, and homes in Goiás where they are said to be the trademark of the state. The husks are available in street markets already folded and ready for stuffing so all you have to do is add the filling.

Pamonhas are made either salty or sweet, fried when they are a day old or baked. The traditional salty version is served with a variety of fillings such as chicken, sausage or palm hearts. The sweet version can be filled with grated coconut and farmers or cream cheese.

You can purchase fresh corn and use the husks for the packets or you can use canned corn and buy a package of cornhusks.

---

30 EARS OF CORN OR 5 (10-OUNCE) CANS OF CORN AND 1 PACKAGE CORN HUSKS

¼ CUP LARD OR BUTTER, MELTED AND KEPT HOT

1 TEASPOON SALT

2 POUNDS BRAZILIAN OR SMOKED ITALIAN SAUSAGE, SLICED

Cut the base off the ears of corn with a sharp knife and carefully remove and reserve the husks. Remove the silk and grate the corn with a grater, scraping off what remains on the cob with a knife. Place the corn in a large bowl with the lard, salt, and sausage, mix well.

Make little packets with the cornhusks (see Note) and fill each packet with about 2 tablespoons of the corn mixture. Tie each end with a wet strip of cornhusk. Fill a pot two-thirds full with water and bring to a boil over high heat. Place the packets in the boiling water and cook until the husks turn yellow, about 20 minutes. Remove the husks from the pot and serve hot with butter and a good cup of coffee.

NOTE: To make packets from the cornhusks, boil the husks to soften them for 5 minutes in water to cover. Discard the tougher outer husks and choose the large inner ones. Fold over the 2 outside edges of each husk so that they join in the middle, fold the husk in half lengthwise to form a small cup. Fill the cup with the corn mixture and tie tightly about 1 inch from the top with strips of the boiled corn husk or string. After the packets are boiled and cooled, they can be stored in the refrigerator for up to 24 hours.

To make fried cream corn, another dish much appreciated in the region, unwrap the boiled corn packet and deep-fry the corn filling in vegetable oil until golden.

Mato Grosso-Style Chicken *with* Manioc Flour

Pirão Mato-Gross
4 SERVINGS

THIS DISH IS PREPARED for women who have just given birth and need nourishment. It is also credited with fortifying a mother's milk.

2 POUNDS SKINLESS AND BONELESS CHICKEN BREASTS	3 TABLESPOONS VEGETABLE OIL
1 TEASPOON SALT	2 CUPS MANIOC FLOUR
2 GARLIC CLOVES, MINCED	

Rinse the chicken breasts, dry, and season them with the salt and garlic. Heat the oil in a deep skillet and fry the chicken until golden on all sides. Cover with water and let simmer for 20 minutes. Remove the pan from the heat, shred the meat and return it to the pan. Add the manioc flour a little at a time, stirring continuously until the mixture resembles meal.

Serve hot.

Dried Beef *with* Manioc

Caribéu

6 SERVINGS

DRIED MEAT, MADE FROM WILD BOAR, which ran in herds in the central lands, had been prepared by the indigenous peoples before the Europeans arrived. In order to preserve their game they drove four forked sticks deeply into the earth forming a tent, on which they placed thick strips of fresh meat. They lit a low fire under the meat, turning it every four hours until it was well roasted, usually about 12 hours. This slow process drew out the juices without toasting the meat, which then became preserved. The Portuguese introduced salt in the late 1700s, as well as cattle, and set up meat processing plants in Rio Grande do Sul. Today, dried beef is consumed nation-wide and adored by Brazilians.

2 POUNDS BRAZILIAN DRIED BEEF
¼ CUP VEGETABLE OIL
2 ONIONS, MINCED
6 GARLIC CLOVES, MINCED
2 POUNDS MANIOC ROOT, PEELED, CORED, AND CUT INTO 1-INCH CUBES
2 TOMATOES, PEELED, SEEDED, AND MINCED

2 GREEN BELL PEPPERS, SEEDED AND CHOPPED
2 RED BELL PEPPERS, SEEDED AND CHOPPED
1 TEASPOON SALT
½ TEASPOON BLACK PEPPER
1 CUP GREEN ONIONS, CHOPPED

Rinse the dried beef and soak it for 6 hours or overnight in the refrigerator. The following day, trim any fat and cut it into 1-inch cubes. Place the beef in a pot, cover with water and bring to a boil. Cook for 10 minutes, covered. Drain and set aside. Heat the oil in a large skillet and sauté the onion and garlic until the onion is translucent. Add the beef cubes and continue sautéing for another 5 minutes. Add the manioc, tomatoes, green and red peppers, salt and black pepper. Add 1 cup water, cover, and simmer for 20 minutes or until the manioc is tender and the sauce thickens. Remove the skillet from the heat and sprinkle with the green onions.

Serve with rice, beans, and *Farofa de Azeite-de-Dendem* (page 40).

Grilled Steaks

Bisteca na Chapa
6 TO 8 SERVINGS

IN THE WORLD AT LARGE when we encounter the word "gaucho," we usually think of the cowboy of the pampas of Argentina. Gaucho also applies to the cattle-raising people of southern Brazil, especially the inhabitants of rural Rio Grande do Sul. Like their Argentine counterparts, the gauchos of southern Brazil are known for their barbecue. Grilled steak is a favorite of gaucho cuisine that has spread throughout Brazil and beyond, and is known as *churrasco*, which translates as "meat grilled on a spit." This process was introduced by the Spaniards who were the first Europeans to arrive in the southern part of South America. This recipe is for beef steaks or slabs of pork that are first marinated and then cooked on a grill over hot coals.

4 POUNDS BEEF STEAKS AND/OR PORK RIBS	1 TO 2 TEASPOONS SALT
1 LARGE ONION, CHOPPED	1 TABLESPOON BLACK PEPPER
4 GARLIC CLOVES, SMASHED	2 TABLESPOONS BUTTER OR LARD, MELTED
1 TABLESPOON WHITE VINEGAR	

Combine the meat with the onion, garlic, vinegar, salt, black pepper, and butter. Let marinate in the refrigerator for 2 hours. Heat a charcoal grill until the coals are white. Place the meat on the grill and brown on both sides or until desired doneness.

Serve with grilled or fried potatoes and a salad.

Fried Beef Tongue *with* Potatoes

Língua de Vaca com Batatinhas

4 SERVINGS

NOT ONLY DO BRAZILIANS use every part of the pig except the squeal, they also use all parts of the cow, even the hoof, in a dish known as *Mocotó*, a Tupi Indian word meaning "hoof." This recipe combines calf's tongue with little potatoes.

2 FRESH CALF'S TONGUES	3 GARLIC CLOVES, MINCED
1 TABLESPOON SALT	3 TABLESPOONS TOMATO PASTE
2 ONIONS, 1 SLICED AND 1 CHOPPED	2 POUNDS SMALL POTATOES, PEELED
¼ CUP VEGETABLE OIL	1 GREEN BELL PEPPER, SEEDED AND
½ CUP CHOPPED FRESH PARSLEY,	CHOPPED
STEMS RESERVED	
½ CUP CHOPPED GREEN ONIONS,	
GREEN PART RESERVED	

Rinse the tongues under warm running water. Soak for 1 hour in cold water. Bring a pot of water to a boil with 2 teaspoons of the salt and the onion slices. Add the tongue, partially cover the pot, and simmer for 1½ hours. Let the tongue cool in the broth. Make a cut in the skin with a sharp knife and peel it off. Trim away any small bones or gristle and cut into cubes.

Heat the oil in a large skillet and sauté the tongue, the remaining 1 teaspoon salt, parsley, green onions, chopped onion, garlic, and tomato paste. When the tongue is golden, add the potatoes and water to cover. Cover the skillet and simmer 15 minutes. Add the green pepper and continue cooking for 5 more minutes.

Place on a large serving platter and sprinkle with the parsley and green onion tips.

Marinated Fish

Escabeche de Pacu
8 SERVINGS

PACU IS A FRESH WATER FISH found in the waters of the Black River in the state of Mato Grosso. It is usually prepared as an *escabeche*, a sauce made of garlic, onions, parsley, cilantro, wine, and olive oil, or coated with cornmeal and fried. *Escabeche* is very popular throughout Brazil, Spain and Portugal. Since *pacu* is not available outside of Brazil you can substitute perch, freshwater catfish, walleye, or tilapia without significantly altering the taste.

FISH:	SAUCE:
3 POUNDS FISH FILLETS, CUT INTO 1-INCH-WIDE STRIPS	6 TABLESPOONS OLIVE OIL
3 TABLESPOONS LIME JUICE	3 GARLIC CLOVES, MINCED
1 TEASPOON SALT	3 ONIONS, THINLY SLICED
½ TEASPOON BLACK PEPPER	1 TEASPOON SALT
1½ CUPS FLOUR	1 JALAPEÑO PEPPER, SEEDED AND MINCED
OIL FOR FRYING	¼ CUP CHOPPED FRESH PARSLEY
	¼ CUP CHOPPED GREEN ONIONS
	½ CUP RED WINE VINEGAR

FOR THE FISH: Place in a shallow dish and season with the lime juice, salt, and pepper and let marinate for 30 minutes. Heat the olive oil in a deep skillet. Remove the fish from the marinade and roll in flour. Shake off excess flour and fry in the hot oil until golden on all sides. Drain on absorbent paper.

FOR THE SAUCE: Heat the olive oil in a skillet and add the garlic and onions, lower the heat, cover and cook until the onions are translucent, stirring occasionally. Add the salt, jalapeño, parsley, green onions, and red wine vinegar, cover and simmer another 10 minutes.

Arrange the fish on a serving platter and cover with the sauce.

NOTE: This dish can be made a day in advance. Place the fried fish in a baking pan, cover with the sauce and refrigerate. The following day reheat in a 350°F oven for 10 minutes or until hot. Serving this the next day gives the flavors a chance to meld.

Mato Grosso-Style Fish

Peixe Mato-grossense
6 SERVINGS

THIS IS A WONDERFUL RECIPE for fish steaks with a banana and pineapple sauce. The dish is very popular in Mato Grosso and the state of Goiás. Fresh water fish is used, but you can substitute any white fish steaks such as grouper, perch, tilapia, or halibut.

4 POUNDS FISH STEAKS	2 CUPS CHOPPED PINEAPPLE
1 CUP FLOUR	3 PALM HEARTS, CUT INTO 1-INCH
OLIVE OIL FOR FRYING	SLICES
3 TABLESPOONS BUTTER	2 TOMATOES, PEELED AND CHOPPED
1 ONION, MINCED	1 TABLESPOON TOMATO PASTE
½ CUP CHOPPED FRESH PARSLEY	1 (14-OUNCE) CAN EVAPORATED MILK
½ CUP CHOPPED GREEN ONIONS	LETTUCE LEAVES FOR GARNISH
1 CUP PITTED BLACK OLIVES	2 POUNDS SWEET POTATO, BOILED
1 TEASPOON SALT	AND PEELED
½ TEASPOON BLACK PEPPER	
2 BANANAS, PEELED AND CUT INTO	
1-INCH SLICES	

Wash the fish steaks, dry with paper towels and coat with the flour, shaking off excess. In a large skillet, heat the oil and fry the fish until golden brown. Set aside. In another skillet melt the butter and sauté the onion, parsley, green onions, and the olives. Add the salt and pepper, bananas, and pineapple. Stir, and add the palm hearts, tomatoes, and tomato paste. Remove from the heat and add the evaporated milk and 1 cup water.

Place the fish on a large serving platter and pour the fruit sauce on top. Decorate the platter with lettuce and serve with sliced boiled sweet potatoes.

Rice *with* Palm Hearts

Arroz com Guariroba

6 SERVINGS

GUARIROBA IS A TYPE OF PALM TREE found in the center-west region. The stalks of the tree are stripped, cut into large pieces and cooked until tender. These palm hearts are slightly bitter, but loved by the people of Mato Grosso, Minas Gerais and Goiás. This particular palm tree which grows to about 60 feet in height is widely cultivated and in great demand. I have substituted canned palm hearts due to the unavailability of the bitter palm heart outside of Brazil.

¼ CUP LARD	3 CUPS RICE
4 GARLIC CLOVES, SMASHED	6 CUPS BOILING WATER
1 (7¾-OUNCE) CAN PALM HEARTS, DRAINED AND SLICED INTO 1-INCH PIECES	1½ TEASPOONS SALT
	½ TEASPOON BLACK PEPPER

In a large skillet, heat 2 tablespoons of the lard and sauté 2 of the garlic cloves and the palm heart slices. Cook over low heat, turning the pieces of palm heart carefully to brown lightly on both sides. Set aside.

Heat the remaining lard and garlic cloves in a medium-size pot and sauté until the garlic is lightly golden. Add the rice and continue sautéing until the rice is also golden, stirring continually. Add the palm hearts and boiling water, mix well. Season with the salt and pepper and cook for about 20 minutes or until the rice is tender.

Serve immediately with grilled meats or fish.

Wealthy Harlot's Rice

Arroz de Puta Rica

8 SERVINGS

THIS TRADITIONAL DISH FROM GOIÁS was originally called *arroz de puta pobre* (poor whore's rice) a recipe that incorporated leftover meat, beans, and rice. The name was changed as more and richer ingredients were added. Today it has become a sophisticated dish and is included on menus for festive occasions and served in a number of restaurants.

¾ POUND BRAZILIAN DRIED BEEF	2 TEASPOONS SALT
4 SLICES BACON, CHOPPED (4 OUNCES)	½ TEASPOON BLACK PEPPER
2 TABLESPOONS OLIVE OIL	6 CUPS BOILING WATER
2 FRESH PORK SAUSAGE LINKS, SLICED	1 CUP CORN KERNELS, FROZEN OR
¼ INCH THICK	CANNED AND DRAINED
4 CHICKEN THIGHS, HALVED	1 CUP PEAS, FROZEN OR CANNED AND
2 SMOKED PORK SAUSAGE LINKS,	DRAINED
SLICED ¼ INCH THICK	½ CUP CHOPPED GREEN OLIVES
4 GARLIC CLOVES, CRUSHED	½ CUP RAISINS
3 CUPS WHITE RICE	

Soak the beef in water to cover for 6 hours or overnight in the refrigerator. The following day, trim the fat and cube the beef.

Place the bacon and the olive oil in a large pot and cook over high heat, stirring, until the bacon is crisp. Add the fresh pork sausage, chicken, and dried beef cubes, and sauté, stirring until the meats are nicely browned. Add the smoked sausage, garlic, and rice, mix well and sauté for another 3 minutes. Add salt and pepper, and the boiling water. Cover the pot, lower the heat, and cook until the meats are tender. Add the corn, peas, olives, raisins, and more water if necessary. Mix well and heat until the vegetables are hot. Place the rice on a large deep platter and serve immediately.

Paraguayan Breakfast Cake

Sopa Paraguaia
MAKES 30 PIECES

IN THE PORTUGUESE LANGUAGE, the title of this recipe translates as Paraguayan soup. It is not really a soup, but a delicious salted cake that is very popular in Paraguay for breakfast. Although the dish originated in the neighboring country of Paraguay it has become a part of the cuisine of the Center-West region of Brazil, another example of the influence of this neighboring country.

½ CUP BUTTER	2 CUPS FRESH FARMER'S CHEESE,
2 LARGE ONIONS, SLICED	COARSELY GRATED
1 QUART MILK, BOILING	5 EGGS, SEPARATED
2 CUPS CORNMEAL	1 TABLESPOON BAKING POWDER
1 TEASPOON SALT	

Preheat the oven to 375°F and grease a 9 x 13-inch pan.

In a medium-size skillet heat the butter and sauté the onions until translucent. Add the boiling milk, mix well and then gradually add the cornmeal, whisking constantly to obtain a smooth batter. Season with salt and remove from heat. Add the cheese and egg yolks and mix well. Beat the egg whites into stiff peaks and add them to the mixture along with the baking powder.

Transfer the mixture to the prepared pan and bake for about 40 minutes until firm and lightly browned. Remove from the oven and let cool about 10 minutes on a rack. Invert and cut into pieces. Serve warm.

Manioc Biscuits

Caburé

10 BISCUITS

THIS IS A QUICK AND EASY RECIPE for biscuits made with grated manioc root and cheese. The unusual ingredient here is the grated manioc root used instead of the flour that we normally use for biscuits, a delicious change of pace.

1¼ POUNDS MANIOC ROOT, PEELED AND GRATED	1 TEASPOON SALT
1 CUP GRATED PARMESAN CHEESE	½ TEASPOON SUGAR
1 EGG	2 TABLESPOONS BUTTER

Preheat the oven to 350°F and lightly grease a baking sheet.

In a large bowl, combine the manioc, cheese, egg, salt, and sugar. Cut in the butter with 2 knives or a pastry blender. Drop tablespoons of batter onto the prepared cookie sheet and bake for about 8 to 10 minutes or until golden.

Cool and serve to accompany any meal with grilled meats or fish.

Mato Grosso Peanut Brittle

Pé-de-moleque mato-grossense
MAKES ABOUT 30 PIECES

MOLEQUE COMES FROM THE KIMBUNDU WORD, *muleke*, which in Angolan means "lad" or "boy." In modern Brazilian Portuguese the word originally had a pejorative connotation, similar to pickaninny in the American South. Today in Brazil, *moleque* means "urchin" or "brat" and is used without regard to color or race. But the name of the dessert derives from its original meaning, black boy. The Portuguese word *pê* translates as foot. Thus, the literal translation of the dessert is "black boy's foot." In contemporary Brazil the term seems to be purged of its mildly pejorative connotation and is thought of, humorously, as "street urchin's foot."

In the center-west region of Brazil this dish is as popular as it is in the northeast where it is said to have originated.

2½ CUPS SUGAR	1½ CUPS WHOLE MILK
2½ CUPS PEANUTS WITHOUT SKINS, TOASTED	1 (14-OUNCE) CAN SWEETENED CONDENSED MILK

In a medium-size pot, heat the sugar, peanuts, and milk over medium heat, stirring constantly with a wooden spoon. When the mixture begins to come away from the sides of the pan, add the sweetened condensed milk, and stir occasionally until the mixture thickens. Remove the pot from the stove and place a tablespoon of the mixture on a buttered marble slab or baking sheet. Let cool and store in covered containers.

Miniature Caramel Tarts

Pastelinho
MAKES ABOUT 40 TARTS

THE DOUGH FOR THESE LITTLE TARTS is similar to that used for the meat and cheese variety from Goiás (page 134). These little tarts appear to be an adaptation of the pastries from the Belém district in Lisbon, Portugal. The Brazilian version, however, is filled with caramel instead of egg custard and the dough includes baking powder. No matter which dough is used, these tarts are delicious.

FILLING:	DOUGH:
4 (14-OUNCE) CANS SWEETENED CONDENSED MILK	4 CUPS FLOUR
	1 CUP PLUS 2 TABLESPOONS BUTTER
	1½ TEASPOONS BAKING POWDER
	1 TEASPOON SALT
	CINNAMON FOR GARNISH

FOR THE FILLING: Place the unopened cans of condensed milk in a large pot. Fill the pot with water to 4 inches above the cans and bring to a boil. Reduce the heat and simmer for 2 hours. Make sure that water remains above the cans as they cook. Remove the cans and let cool for 30 minutes before opening.

FOR THE DOUGH: Place the flour in a large bowl and cut in the butter until the mixture resembles a coarse meal. Add ½ cup water, mix well, and knead until a dough forms.

Preheat the oven to 350°F. Roll out the dough ⅛ inch thick and cut out 5-inch circles. Line muffin tins with the dough and crimp the edges. Prick the dough with a fork. Place the muffin tin in the oven for 10 minutes to lightly brown the dough. Remove from the oven and fill each tin two-thirds full, with about 2 tablespoons of filling. Return to the oven for about 10 minutes to melt the caramel. Remove from oven and sprinkle with cinnamon.

Cool and serve.

Southern Cuisine

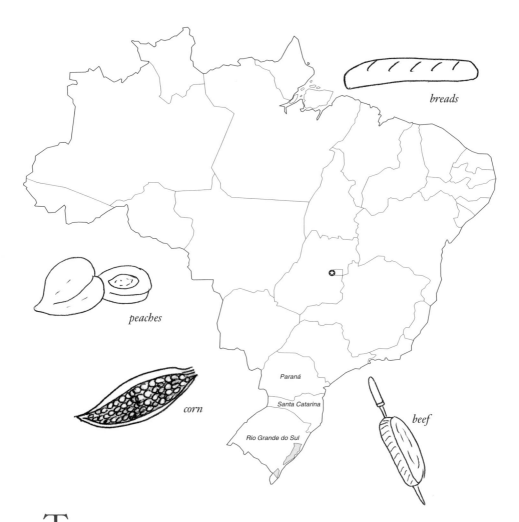

breads

peaches

corn

Paraná

Santa Catarina

Rio Grande do Sul

beef

The southern region comprises the states of Paraná, Santa Catarina, and Rio Grande do Sul. Its cuisine has been especially influenced by immigrants from Germany and Italy. Rio Grande do Sul is known for the legendary gaucho or southern cowboy who gave Brazil the *churrasco*—meat grilled over hot coals. The state is also known for its good wines.

The original inhabitants of the area that today is the state of Rio Grande do Sul were the Tapuia Indians who lived in the grasslands and the Guaranis who lived along the coast. The Indians also played a role in establishing the custom of making *churrascos*. They were the first to grill the meat from their hunt, such as fish, snakes, monkeys, and lizards, on sticks over a fire, a custom that has spread throughout the country. Beef, now the favorite barbecue meat, was only introduced in 1682, when the first cattle arrived, as well as the first horses, brought from the south across the Uruguay River. In the beginning every part of the cattle was used—hides for clothing, horns and bones for utensils, but the meat, considered worthless, was distributed to the cowhands. It was only in the early nineteenth century that beef came to have any commercial value. Cattle ranches prospered and Rio Grande do Sul was soon supplying beef to all of Brazil.

By the 1600s Spanish Jesuits had arrived in the eastern part of the state to establish missions and the Portuguese had settled along the coast. Thus the first gaucho is believed to have been of Indian, Spanish, and Portuguese ancestry. Germans immigrants arrived in the 1800s, and began to cultivate the potato. They introduced the processes of smoking meats, sausagemaking, and the practice of afternoon coffee with various breads, cakes, and pastries. Today the two largest cities in the mountainous region are Gramado and Canela, where one finds many dishes of Italian and German origin.

Italian immigrants also began arriving around 1875 and settled in the mountainous region. They found the climate similar to that of their homeland, dry and cool, and thus ideal for planting vineyards. Today the region is the largest producer of wine in the country. Besides wine, the Italians also brought polenta, risotto, pasta, and sausagemaking techniques. The most popular pastas are spaghetti and fusilli, served with a lean meat sauce, chicken, or sausage. The climate that attracted the Italians and Germans, if not enriched the culinary customs of the indigenous people. Southern cuisine, as we know it, is today a combination of foods from northern Europe, the Mediterranean, and lest we forget the northeast of Brazil, where *charque* (dried beef), for example, originated and is today one of the most typical dishes of Rio Grande. Despite all of these outside influences, two traditions that originated in this area continue to be favorites of the gauchos: the *churrasco* (meats on the grill) and *chimarrão* or *mate* (a tea drink). *Chimarrão*, from the Spanish *cimarrón*, is to the gaucho what a demitasse coffee is to the people of São Paulo—a symbol of hospitality. The custom of drinking *mate* is common to Paraguay, Argentina, Uruguay, Chile, and Brazil where it took root in the states of Rio Grande do Sul, Santa Catarina, Paraná, and Mato Grosso, where it is more often served cold because of the hot climate. It is a ritualistic beverage, served in a gourd, which is passed from person to person and the same *bomba* (a straw like device usually made of silver with a gold mouthpiece used to drink the tea) is passed from person to person. This is a sign of trust, peace, understanding, and brotherhood.

Constantly on the move, herding cattle the gauchos didn't have time to stop and prepare complete meals; hence the *churrasco* was born. A gaúcho would kill a steer and cook it directly over a fire or cut into pieces and skewer it with small branches and suspend those pieces of wood over a fire. These cowboys used almost every part of the ox. It's still very common to find dishes made from tongue, liver, giblets, and tripe.

Rice also plays an important role in the diet of the gaúcho and is prepared in a variety of ways: with collards, cabbage, chicken, tripe, and occasionally with peaches. The most famous dish is *arroz-de-carreteiro*, or rice with dried beef. Rice also accompanies most bean dishes.

Corn on the cob is especially appreciated when roasted over coals or cut into pieces for soup or stews. Dried corn (*canjica*) is cooked with chicken or dried beef. Manioc, potatoes, sweet potatoes, green beans, and chayote are eaten as side dishes or used in soups.

The sweets consumed were a mixture of traditional desserts from Portugal and other European countries, principally Germany, with its rich torts. But it was the gauchos, the first Brazilians, who experienced a new treat: ice cream in the beginning of the seventeenth century. Thanks to the cold winters, they used the snow to prepare this delicious dessert. With the passage of time, new influences led to slight changes in the cuisine. New vegetables, elaborate desserts, and fruits cooked in syrup became part of the cuisine. Even the traditional *churrasco*, came to include new cuts of meat such as pork loin, fillet mignon, *picanha* (shredded beef), and sausages.

Brazilian Sauce

Molho Brasileiro
MAKES 1 CUP

THIS SAUCE IS USED TO MOISTEN roasted or grilled beef, pork, chicken or fish. It is also used as a dressing for lettuce salads.

1 SMALL ONION, THINLY SLICED	½ CUP OLIVE OIL
1 TOMATO, THINLY SLICED	2 TABLESPOONS WHITE VINEGAR
1 CUP CILANTRO LEAVES	SALT AND BLACK PEPPER

Place the onions in a bowl. Pour boiling water over them and let stand for 1 minute. Drain the onions and let cool. Mix with the remaining ingredients and serve.

NOTE: Brazilians believe that scalding the onions for 1 minute removes the acid and makes them more digestible.

Red Pepper Antipasto

Antepasto de Pimentão à Gaúcho

12 SERVINGS

WE CAN THANK ITALIAN IMMIGRANTS for introducing this wonderful appetizer in Brazil. It only takes one hour to put together and is great served with a glass of wine before dinner.

12 RED BELL PEPPERS, SEEDED AND CUT INTO WIDE STRIPS	1 TEASPOON DRY OREGANO
1 CUP SUNFLOWER OIL	1 BAY LEAF
2 BEEF BOUILLON CUBES	½ TEASPOON BLACK PEPPER
½ CUP HOT WATER	½ CUP RED WINE VINEGAR
1 MEDIUM ONION, MINCED	OLIVE OIL

Preheat the oven to 400°F. Place the pepper strips on a baking pan, sprinkle with 2 tablespoons of the sunflower oil and bake for 1 hour or until soft.

Meanwhile, dissolve the beef bouillon in the hot water. Heat the remaining sunflower oil in a skillet, sauté the onion, adding the oregano, bay leaf, black pepper, and broth. Add the vinegar and the peppers. When the peppers are cooked, place the mixture on a serving platter and pour the sauce on top. Drizzle olive oil over the platter and serve immediately.

NOTE: If possible, prepare this dish the day before to give the flavors a chance to meld. It will be a much more delicious dish.

Potato Omelet

Omelete com Batatas

4 SERVINGS

SPANISH IMMIGRANTS introduced a number of dishes to Brazil that have become a part of the southern cuisine. This omelet made with potatoes and onions is similar to the Spanish *tortilla* and is now enjoyed throughout Brazil.

¼ CUP PLUS 3 TABLESPOONS OLIVE OIL	1 SMALL ONION, THINLY SLICED
1 POUND SMALL WHITE BOILING POTATOES, PEELED AND THINLY SLICED	6 EGGS
	SALT AND BLACK PEPPER

Heat ¼ cup of the oil in a large skillet and cook the potatoes and onions over low heat turning with a spatula until the potatoes are tender.

Meanwhile, in a bowl, beat eggs with salt and pepper to taste and add the potato mixture. In the same skillet, heat 2 tablespoons of the remaining oil over high heat and pour in the potato mixture. Lower the heat and stir gently with a wooden spoon. Cook over low heat until the eggs set. Place a plate over the skillet and flip the omelet onto the plate. Add the remaining 1 tablespoon of oil to the pan, heat, and slide the omelet back into the pan. Cook until the underside is golden.

Serve hot or at room temperature.

Rice Balls

Bolinhos de Arroz

6 SERVINGS

THESE RICE BALLS ARE GREAT served as an appetizer or side dish with grilled meats and are appreciated throughout the Portuguese-speaking world. In Rio de Janeiro, sardines and cheese are added for an unusual taste. In Portugal, flaked fish is added. Prepare the rice the day before serving because it has to be cooked again the following the day to obtain the desired consistency.

2 CUPS COOKED RICE	½ CUP CHOPPED ONION
2 CUPS WHOLE MILK	SALT
1 TABLESPOON BAKING POWDER	1 CUP FLOUR
½ CUP CHOPPED FRESH PARSLEY	VEGETABLE OIL OR LARD FOR FRYING
½ CUP CHOPPED GREEN ONIONS	

Place the rice in a pot with water to cover, and cook for 20 minutes, or until the water has evaporated. Mix in the milk and add the baking powder, parsley, green onions, onion, 1 cup water, and salt. If the mixture is too wet, add the flour, a little at a time, until the mixture becomes stiff.

In a deep skillet, heat the oil 3 inches deep to 350°F. Form the mixture into balls the size of a walnut and fry in the hot oil until golden on all sides. Drain on paper towels and set aside until all the mixture is used.

Serve warm.

NOTE: Test the consistency of the mixture by frying 1 ball. If the ball falls apart, add another egg.

Gaucho Meatballs

Almôndegas à Moda Gaúcho
4 SERVINGS

THIS DISH IS A PORTUGUESE AND ITALIAN culinary combination. These meatballs are made from both dried beef and salt cod. These two ingredients have to be soaked overnight to be ready for this recipe.

8 OUNCES DRIED BRAZILIAN BEEF	1 MEDIUM ONION, MINCED
8 OUNCES SKINLESS AND	1 TABLESPOON FLOUR
BONELESS SALT COD	2 TABLESPOONS WARM MILK
1 TABLESPOON CHOPPED FRESH	(OPTIONAL)
PARSLEY	VEGETABLE OIL FOR FRYING
1 GREEN PEPPER, CHOPPED	

Soak the dried beef and salt cod separately in water to cover for at least 6 hours or overnight. The following day remove the beef and cod from the water and rinse each well. Remove all the fat from beef and cut into cubes. Cut the cod into small pieces and grind both the cod and beef in a meat grinder or in a food processor. Place the mixture in a large bowl and add the parsley, green pepper, onion, and flour. Mix well. If the mixture does not come together, add the warm milk.

Heat the oil in a deep skillet. Spoon a small amount of the mixture into your hands and roll to form balls the size of golfballs. Repeat until all of the mixture is used. Fry the balls in hot oil and drain on paper towels.

Serve with toothpicks as an appetizer.

Mango Soup

Sopa de Manga
4 SERVINGS

THIS DELICIOUS COLD SOUP is enjoyed in the state of Rio Grande do Sul, especially during the warmer months. It is usually served in clay mugs and sometimes topped with a dollop of whipped cream.

1 LARGE MANGO, PEELED AND CHOPPED	6 CUPS ICE WATER
1½ CUBES CHICKEN BOUILLON	1 TEASPOON SALT
1 CUP BOILING WATER	½ TEASPOON BLACK PEPPER

Place the mango in a blender and purée. Dissolve the chicken bouillon cubes in the boiling water. Pour the ice water, chicken bouillon, and the mango purée into a plastic or glass container. Season with the salt and black pepper, mix well and refrigerate for at least 4 hours.

Serve cold.

Shrimp Soup

Caldo de Camarões
8 SERVINGS

THIS SOUP IS A MUST for shrimp lovers. It is a delicately flavored shrimp broth enhanced with whole shrimp. Santa Catarina borders on the ocean and its waters abound with seafood, especially shrimp. They are eaten fried, breaded, steamed, and grilled, but this is one of the tastiest ways to prepare them.

4 POUNDS JUMBO SHRIMP	2 LARGE TOMATOES, PEELED, SEEDED,
2 TEASPOONS SALT	AND FINELY CHOPPED
2 LARGE ONIONS, CUT INTO EIGHTHS	⅓ CUP OLIVE OIL
A FEW DROPS HOT SAUCE	8 FRESH BASIL LEAVES
JUICE OF 1 LIME	½ TEASPOON WHITE PEPPER
	½ CUP MANIOC FLOUR

Wash, peel and devein the shrimp. Place 8 of the shrimp in a pot with 3 cups water and 1 teaspoon of the salt. Bring to a boil, lower the heat and simmer for 1 minute. Cover and remove from the heat. When the shrimp are cool, remove them from the water, reserving the broth, and place them in a blender with 1½ cups of the broth, the onion, and hot sauce. Purée the mixture and set aside. Place the remaining shrimp in a large bowl, season with the lime juice and remaining 1 teaspoon of salt. Mix well and let sit for 20 minutes.

In a large pot, place the tomatoes, olive oil, basil, and the puréed shrimp mixture. Cook over low heat stirring constantly for about 15 minutes adding the remaining broth a little at a time so as not to stop the simmering. Season the mixture with the white pepper. Add the remaining shrimp and continue simmering until the shrimp are cooked or turn pink. Remove the shrimp with a slotted spoon from the pot and set aside. Bring the broth to a boil and slowly add the manioc flour, whisking constantly to prevent lumps. Pour the hot broth into 8 soup bowls and garnish with the whole shrimp.

Chicken Creole

Galinha Crioula

4 SERVINGS

GALINHA CRIOULA IS SIMILAR to a dish of Portuguese origin that I sampled on the island of São Tomé, in the Gulf of Guinea off the west coast of Africa. It is a rice dish made with leftover fish, poultry, or meat. In most of Brazil *crioulo* and its feminine form *crioula* generally refer to people of African descent, but in Rio Grande do Sul the term applies to any native of the state as well as to a common fowl. This recipe from Rio Grande do Sul combines the two meanings.

1 (4- TO 5-POUND) CHICKEN	3 TOMATOES, PEELED AND SEEDED
¼ CUP LARD OR VEGETABLE OIL	SALT
2 ONIONS, CHOPPED	1 TABLESPOON BUTTER
2 GARLIC CLOVES, MINCED	1½ CUPS RICE
1 GREEN BELL PEPPER, SEEDED AND CHOPPED	½ CUP GRATED PARMESAN CHEESE

Wash the chicken and cut it into 8 pieces. Melt the lard in a large pan and sauté the chicken over medium heat, turning until golden on all sides. Add the onion, garlic, and green pepper, stir and cook for another 5 minutes. Add the tomatoes, salt, and water to cover the chicken. Simmer until the chicken is cooked through and the water has almost evaporated.

MEANWHILE PREPARE THE RICE: place 3 cups water, the butter, and the rice in a pot. Bring to a boil, cover and cook for 20 minutes or until all water has been absorbed.

Preheat the oven to 350°F and grease a 9 x 11-inch baking dish. Mix the rice with the chicken and place it in the prepared baking pan. Sprinkle with the Parmesan cheese and brown in the oven. The dish is ready when the top is lightly golden. Serve hot.

Grilled Squabs on Skewers

Galeto

4 SERVINGS

IT IS SAID THAT ITALIAN IMMIGRANTS were responsible for introducing *galeto* to southern Brazil. This young chicken is usually 20 to 25 days old and weighs about one pound. These chickens are similar to the small game birds found in Italy. There are many restaurants in the south of Brazil that specialize in this tasty dish of grilled chickens usually accompanied by some type of pasta topped with a tomato sauce and a salad of chicory, onions, and green peppers. This dish should be started the day before so that the chickens can marinate overnight.

I have substituted squab for the young chickens as they approximate the size.

6 SQUABS OR ROCK CORNISH GAME HENS (6 POUNDS)	2 TABLESPOONS CHOPPED GREEN ONIONS
2 ONIONS, QUARTERED	1 TABLESPOON CHOPPED FRESH SAGE
6 GARLIC CLOVES	2 SPRIGS OF MARJORAM, STEMMED
3 CUPS WHITE WINE	½ TEASPOON GROUND NUTMEG
2 TABLESPOONS CHOPPED FRESH PARSLEY	1 TEASPOON SALT
	½ TEASPOON BLACK PEPPER

Butterfly the squabs by cutting down the breast bone, but don't cut in half (it should remain in a single piece). Open out and press flat in a deep roasting pan. Place the onions, garlic, wine, parsley, green onions, sage, marjoram, nutmeg, salt and black pepper in a blender or food processor. Blend to a purée. Pour the purée over the squabs, making sure that they are well coated on all sides. Refrigerate overnight so that the marinade penetrates the squabs.

The following day remove the squabs from the marinade. Heat a charcoal grill to hot and place the squabs over the coals on the grill. Grill, basting occasionally with the marinade until the squabs are cooked (about 5 to 8 minutes on each side). Turn occasionally. Serve at a barbecue with other grilled meats.

NOTE: If a grill is not available, preheat oven to 450°F. Place the squabs in a greased pan and roast for 20 to 30 minutes basting twice with the marinade. Roast until the skin is dark brown. Remove from the oven and serve.

Beef Stew

Puchero

12 SERVINGS

PUCHERO IS A DELICIOUS BEEF STEW very popular in the southern region. It includes a variety of meats and vegetables, and is served with a manioc purée. The original recipe calls for breast meat from the ox but, you can substitute lean chuck or beef rump. This recipe makes enough to serve a small crowd.

3 TABLESPOONS SALT
6 ONIONS, QUARTERED
6 TOMATOES, PEELED
2 GREEN BELL PEPPERS, SEEDED AND QUARTERED
2 SMALL HOT GREEN PEPPERS, HALVED
6 POUNDS BEEF CHUCK OR RUMP, CUBED
2 POUNDS SMOKED SAUSAGE (*LINGÜIÇA*), CUT INTO 2-INCH SLICES
2 POUNDS SWEET POTATOES, QUARTERED
4 CARROTS, PEELED AND QUARTERED
6 EARS CORN, QUARTERED

1 BUNCH TURNIP GREENS, STEMMED
5 CHAYOTES, PEELED AND QUARTERED
2 POUNDS MANIOC ROOT, PEELED, HALVED, AND CUT INTO 2-INCH SLICES
2 POUNDS PUMPKIN OR BUTTERNUT SQUASH, PEELED AND CUT INTO 2-INCH PIECES
2 POUNDS WHITE POTATOES, PEELED AND HALVED
1 HEAD CAULIFLOWER, FLORETS ONLY
2 CUPS MANIOC FLOUR
½ CUP GREEN ONIONS, CHOPPED

Place a 6-quart pot over medium heat and fill halfway with water. Add the salt, onions, tomatoes, bell peppers, and hot peppers and bring to a boil. Add the beef and sausage, lower the heat and continue cooking for another 20 minutes. Add the sweet potatoes, carrots, corn, turnip greens, chayote, and manioc. Continue cooking for another 20 minutes then add the pumpkin and potatoes. Lastly, add the cauliflower. When all the vegetables are tender, another 5 minutes, remove with a slotted spoon and slowly pour the manioc flour into the broth, stirring constantly to prevent lumps. Return the vegetables and meats to the broth, mix well and serve in a large deep platter, sprinkled with the green onion.

NOTE: Many cooks also add cabbage (quartered) to this dish. If you don't have a large platter, separate the meat from the vegetables when serving.

Brazilian Barbecue

Churrasco

8 SERVINGS

THE *CHURRASCO* IS A SPECIALTY of the southern Brazilian cowboy (gaucho), and there are many ways to cook and eat this "dish." The tradition has absorbed the habits and customs of the diverse society. For example, the German colony eats their barbecue with *cuca* (page 178), a cake prepared with eggs, butter, and yeast. The Italians introduced sausages, young chickens, and the spit or skewer. The cowboys, because of their Spanish heritage, roast meat on a grill: the original *churrasco*.

In the open plains, the cowboy's daily barbecue consists of sheep, unlike the city cowboy who prefers beef. Nationwide, the favorite barbecue meat is also beef, but people from Rio Grande do Sul eat both beef and mutton. The most popular cuts, during the week, are ribs, the breast bone, and the fibrous meat that covers ribs (*matambre*). On weekends you will find flank steak, tenderloin, sausage, and chicken grilling over coals. The only seasoning used is coarse salt, which seals in the juices and lends a very special flavor.

½ CUP SEA SALT OR KOSHER SALT   4 POUNDS PORK (RIBS)
4 POUNDS BEEF (RIBS, FLANK STEAK
  WITH SOME FAT)

Prepare the grill by heating the coals to hot (white). Sprinkle salt over the ribs and flank steak and place on the grill. The meat should be at least 6 inches from the fire. Place bone side down. When the underside is done turn over so that the fat side is over the fire. Remove from the fire as soon as each piece is done to the desired doneness. Let the meat sit for about 10 minutes to seal in the juices, and cut into serving pieces.

Serve with salads, rice, fried manioc, and Toasted Manioc Flour (page 40).

NOTE: You can prepare a mixed grill by adding sausages and chicken. If using sausages, prick them before placing them on the grill.

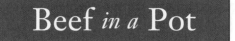

Beef *in a* Pot

Barreada

10 SERVINGS

LEGEND HAS IT that more than 200 years ago in the coastal highlands of the state of Paraná, *Barreada* was served by the locals during carnival to give them energy so they could dance all night without tiring. The dish was traditionally prepared over a slow wood fire in a sealed clay pot for 18 to 24 hours. To obtain a similar result, place the ingredients in a crock pot at the lowest setting and simmer for at least 15 hours. If you don't have a crock pot see the Note below for an alternative method.

1 POUND SLICED BACON	2 TEASPOONS GROUND CUMIN
2 TOMATOES, PEELED AND SEEDED	2 TEASPOONS DRIED OREGANO
2 ONIONS	1 TABLESPOON SALT
2 CELERY STALKS, CHOPPED	2 TABLESPOONS TOMATO PASTE
3 LEEKS, CHOPPED, WHITE PARTS ONLY	3 BAY LEAVES
	6 CLOVES GARLIC, CHOPPED
1 CUP CHOPPED FRESH PARSLEY	½ TEASPOON GROUND NUTMEG
1 CUP CHOPPED GREEN ONIONS	3 TABLESPOONS WHITE VINEGAR
6 POUNDS STEW BEEF, CUBED	1 COLLARD GREEN LEAF

In a large bowl place the tomatoes, onions, celery, leeks, parsley, and green onions, mix well. In the crock pot, spread a layer of bacon. Cover with a layer of the vegetable mixture and then a layer of the beef. Repeat these layers including any juice. Sprinkle with the cumin, oregano, salt, and nutmeg. With a mortar and pestle crush the garlic with the bay leaves and add the tomato paste. Spread this mixture over the top and sprinkle with the vinegar. Cut the collard green leaf into a circle a little larger than the diameter of the crock and place on top. Place the cover on the crock and weigh it down with a heavy object such as a brick or iron skillet so that no steam escapes. Do not open for the first 15 hours.

Allow the beef to cook for 15 to 18 hours. Serve in ceramic bowls with rice, banana slices, Toasted Manioc Flour (page 40), and hot sauce. The people from Paraná enjoy a *caipirinha* (page 85) or a cold beer with this dish.

NOTE: If a crock pot is not available, place all ingredients in a large pot and place an aluminum plate or baking sheet between the heat and the pot and cook over the lowest heat available. Place a heavy object on the lid to keep steam from escaping and cook following the directions above.

Roast Pork *with* Sweet Potatoes

Filé de Porco com Batata-Doce

6 SERVINGS

THIS COMBINATION OF PORK AND SWEET POTATOES is unique and delicious. Be sure that the pork has enough fat so that it remains moist during cooking. Serve with boiled white rice and green beans.

2 POUNDS SWEET POTATOES	SALT
3 POUNDS BONELESS PORK LOIN	WHITE PEPPER
ROAST WITH THIN LAYER OF FAT,	JUICE OF 2 LEMONS
SLICED 1-INCH THICK	

Preheat the oven to 350°F.

Place the sweet potatoes in water to cover over high heat. Bring to a boil, reduce the heat, and cook for 15 minutes. Remove from the water, cool, peel, and cut into 1-inch slices. Set aside. Layer the slices of pork in a roasting pan and season with salt, white pepper, and the lemon juice. Bake until the pork begins to brown, about 15 minutes. Add the sweet potatoes and continue baking for 20 minutes. Baste occasionally with the pan drippings. If none exists, use a little oil. When the pork is cooked, the dish is ready.

Serve with a nice red wine.

Catfish Stew

Bagre Ensopado

6 SERVINGS

IN THE NORTHEAST most *ensopados* are stews made with chicken and coconut. This version from the south does not call for coconut milk and is made with fish. It's a southern-style *moqueca*. The fish commonly used in the south is *bagre* (catfish). If catfish is not available, you can substitute halibut.

1 LARGE CATFISH, CUT INTO STEAKS OR 6 HALIBUT STEAKS (ABOUT 4 POUNDS)	1 (14-OUNCE) CAN CORN, DRAINED
	1 RED BELL PEPPER, SEEDED AND QUARTERED
SALT	1 BAY LEAF
4 GARLIC CLOVES, MINCED	½ CUP CHOPPED FRESH PARSLEY
1 BUNCH COLLARD GREENS, STEMMED	½ CUP WHITE WINE
4 MEDIUM ONIONS, SLICED	½ CUP OLIVE OIL
4 TOMATOES, SLICED	

Remove the skin from the catfish and season with the salt and garlic. Line a large deep pot with collard greens. Top with the onion and tomato and sprinkle with half of the corn. Season with salt and layer half the fish steaks on top. Cover with a few collard green leaves, the red pepper, and a bay leaf. Repeat the layers ending with collard greens. Pour the wine and olive oil over the dish, place the pot over low heat and simmer for 1 hour.

NOTE: This dish is usually served with a *pirão* (page 140). To prepare the *pirão* bring the broth from the dish to a boil. Sprinkle half the same amount of manioc flour into the broth and, using a whisk, stir until the mixture is smooth. Cook over low heat for 5 minutes, stirring constantly.

Baked Stuffed Fish

Tainha na Telha

6 SERVINGS

THIS RECIPE MAY HAVE come from the Ribatejo region of Portugal where a similar dish made with freshwater fish is popular. In Portugal the fish is baked between two roof tiles with onions and bacon. In Santa Catarina and other states in southern Brazil, because of the large Italian population, it is very possible that the Italian word for a baking dish, *teglia*, may have been translated by the Portuguese to *telha* which means roof tile. This dish can be prepared in a shallow clay baking dish and not lose any of its original flavor.

FISH:	¼ CUP CHOPPED GREEN ONIONS
1 WHOLE FISH, ABOUT 6 POUNDS	1 POUND SMALL SHRIMP, SHELLED
(BLUEFISH, GROUPER OR MACKEREL),	AND DEVEINED
CLEANED	1 CUP MANIOC FLOUR
JUICE OF 1 LIME	6 BLACK OLIVES, CHOPPED
SALT AND BLACK PEPPER	1 TEASPOON SALT
1 TABLESPOON GROUND SAGE	
	GARNISH:
FILLING:	24 SMALL BOILING POTATOES, PEELED
3 TABLESPOONS OLIVE OIL	1 LARGE ONION, THINLY SLICED
1 ONION, CHOPPED	1 LARGE TOMATO, THINLY SLICED
¼ CUP CHOPPED FRESH PARSLEY	

Place the fish in a bowl with the lime juice, salt, pepper, and sage. Set aside in the refrigerator.

Preheat the oven to 350°F. Grease a baking dish large enough to hold the fish. In a large skillet, heat the oil over high heat. Add the onions, parsley, and green onions, reduce the heat and sauté until the onions are soft. Add the shrimp and continue to sauté, stirring until the shrimp are barely cooked, then add the manioc flour and olives. Season with salt and stir until the mixture resembles coarse meal. Stuff the fish with the mixture and place in the prepared pan and bake for 30 minutes.

While the fish is baking, place the potatoes in a pot with salted water to cover. Bring to a boil, lower the heat and cook the potatoes for 15 minutes. Pour off the water. Remove the fish from the oven, cover with the potatoes, tomatoes, and onion rings. Return to the oven for another 15 minutes or until fish flakes easily.

Place the fish on a large serving platter, cover with the potatoes, tomatoes, and onions and serve with white rice.

NOTE: In Santa Catarina, the preferred fish is mullet. In the United States, mullet only grows to an average of about 3 pounds, so I have used snapper and bluefish in this recipe.

Mashed Pumpkin *with* Corn Flour

Quibebe

4 SERVINGS

QUIBEBE IS VERY POPULAR among the Gaúcho people, and it is usually served with grilled meats. Pumpkin is traditional, but you can substitute butternut squash if it is not available. The original recipe also calls for bacon, but you can eliminate the bacon to prepare a vegetarian dish.

2 POUNDS FRESH PUMPKIN OR BUTTERNUT SQUASH	SALT
	CHILI POWDER OR CAYENNE PEPPER
2 TABLESPOONS VEGETABLE OIL	1 TEASPOON SUGAR
1 ONION, MINCED	2 TABLESPOONS CORN FLOUR
2 GARLIC CLOVES, MINCED	¼ CUP MINCED PARSLEY

Peel the pumpkin, remove the seeds, and cut into 1-inch cubes. Heat the oil in a medium-size pot and add the pumpkin, garlic, and onions and stir for a few minutes. Add salt to taste, the chili powder, sugar, and 1 cup water and mix well. Lower the heat to a simmer and cook until the pumpkin is soft and almost a purée. Add the corn flour and mix well. Remove from the heat and place in a serving dish. Sprinkle with parsley and serve.

NOTE: If you wish to add bacon, cook 4 slices of bacon in a skillet until crisp. Drain on paper towels and crumble. Add the bacon with the corn flour and mix well.

Rice *with* Sausage

Arroz com Lingüiça

6 SERVINGS

THIS RICE IS ALSO CALLED *arroz de China pobre* (poor China rice). *China pobre* is a gaucho term that refers to "women of the street." In other words, it refers to a degrading life, working at night, sleeping late, waking up famished and going to the store for a quick meal: a few ounces of ground beef, a little manioc flour, a link of sausage, a pat of lard, and an armful of firewood. This gave a stigma to all dishes that were easy and quick to prepare with few ingredients, and they were called *China Pobre*.

2 TABLESPOONS LARD OR VEGETABLE OIL	2 CUPS RICE
	4 CUPS BOILING WATER
1½ POUNDS SMOKED SAUSAGE (*LINGÜIÇA*), CUT INTO 1-INCH SLICES	1 TEASPOON SALT
3 GARLIC CLOVES, THINLY SLICED	

Heat the lard in a large skillet over medium heat. Sauté the sausage and garlic until the sausage is lightly browned. Add the rice, stir, and sauté until the rice is lightly golden. Add the boiling water and the salt. Cover the skillet, reduce the heat to a simmer and cook for about 20 minutes or until the water has been absorbed.

Serve warm.

Rice *with* Peaches

Arroz com Pêssagos
6 SERVINGS

RICE WITH PEACHES is an unusual, but delicious combination. It is quick to prepare and calls for few ingredients. Cooks in Rio Grande do Sul serve it as an accompaniment to chicken, pork, or grilled meats.

1½ CUPS RICE	6 PEACHES, PEELED, PITTED, AND
1 TEASPOON SALT	SLICED

In a medium-size pot, bring the rice, 3 cups water, and 1 teaspoon salt to a boil, cover, and reduce the heat. Cook for 10 minutes, add the peaches, stir, cover and cook for another 10 minutes or until the water has been absorbed.

Serve with grilled meats.

Mule-Driver's Rice

Arroz de Carreteiro

6 SERVINGS

THE WORD *CARRETEIRO* comes from Spanish and means "driver of an ox cart or wagon." The dish got its name because these drivers, who were gone for long periods of time, took food on the trail that wouldn't spoil, such as dried beef. When they stopped to eat they would prepare rice to which they added the dried beef.

Today this dish is still served for parties and family gatherings. Each cook has her or his own recipe and this is one version of many. Begin preparing this dish the day before serving because the dried beef has to soak overnight.

1 POUND BRAZILIAN DRIED BEEF	2 CUPS RICE
2 TABLESPOONS VEGETABLE OIL	4 CUPS BOILING WATER
1 ONION, MINCED	1 TEASPOON SALT

Wash the dried beef and place in a pot with water to cover. Bring the water to a boil and cook for 5 minutes. Remove the beef and place in a bowl with cold water to cover. Place the bowl in the refrigerator and let stand for 6 hours or overnight. The following day, remove the beef from the water, remove all the fat and shred into bite-size pieces.

In a large pan heat the oil and sauté the onion until translucent. Stir in the dried beef and rice, add the boiling water and salt. Cover the pan, lower the heat, and simmer for about 20 minutes.

Serve as a main dish with a salad or to accompany a dish of mixed beans.

German Banana Sweet Bread

Cuca de Banana Alemã
MAKES 1 LOAF

CUCAS ARE SWEET BREADS that German immigrants brought to Brazil in the 1800s. They have a streusel topping and a variety of fillings, such as banana, raisins, or apples. This recipe calls for a banana filling. The end result is similar to our coffee cake.

4 EGGS, SEPARATED	TOPPING:
2 CUPS SUGAR	6 TABLESPOONS SUGAR
3 TABLESPOONS BUTTER	½ CUP FLOUR
2 CUPS FLOUR	3 TABLESPOONS BUTTER, AT ROOM
1 CUP CORNSTARCH	TEMPERATURE
1 TABLESPOON BAKING POWDER	2 TABLESPOONS GROUND CINNAMON
¾ CUP MILK	
¼ CUP BRANDY	
½ TEASPOON SALT	
4 TO 5 SMALL BANANAS, PEELED AND	
HALVED LENGTHWISE	

Preheat the oven to 350°F. Grease a 9 x 5-inch loaf pan.

Beat the egg yolks with the sugar until pale yellow. Add the butter and continue beating. Slowly add the flour, cornstarch, and baking powder, stirring after each addition. Stir in the milk and the brandy.

Beat the whites and salt until stiff peaks form. Fold into the egg yolk mixture. Pour the dough into the prepared pan. Place the bananas on top of the dough.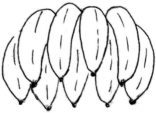

FOR THE TOPPING: mix together the sugar, flour, butter, and cinnamon forming a crumbly mixture. Sprinkle over top of the dough. Bake for 30 minutes or until a toothpick comes out clean.

Getúlio Vargas Pudding

Pudim Getúlio Vargas

8 SERVINGS

THIS DESSERT WAS NAMED FOR GETÚLIO VARGAS from the state of Rio Grande do Sul, president of Brazil from 1930–1945 and 1951–1954. Vargas was fond of pineapple and coconut. Because of this love, this dessert was invented by a baker and given Vargas' name. Today it is popular nationwide.

12 EGGS	1 (8-OUNCE) CAN PINEAPPLE SLICES IN
4 CUPS SUGAR	SYRUP, DRAINED AND CHOPPED
1 CUP GRATED FRESH COCONUT	

Preheat the oven to 350°F. Grease a 9-inch angel food cake pan.

Beat the eggs into a large bowl. Add the sugar and continue beating until the mixture is frothy. Fold in the coconut and pineapple. Pour the batter into the prepared pan and bake until the mixture is golden, about 40 minutes. Chill and serve.

Orange Pudding

Pudim de Laranja
8 SERVINGS

THIS DESSERT COMBINES the Portuguese influence of egg-based desserts with sugar from the plantations of the northeast of Brazil and oranges from the farms.

3 CUPS SUGAR	1 CUP ORANGE JUICE
12 EGGS	

Preheat the oven to 400°F.

In a small pot over low heat, heat 1 cup of the sugar, stirring constantly with a wooden spoon, until it melts and is free of lumps. When the sugar turns a light caramel color, remove it from the heat and pour into a 6-cup mold. Let cool.

In a large bowl beat the eggs, remaining sugar, and orange juice until fluffy. Strain this mixture twice through cheesecloth for a smooth pudding. Pour the batter into the mold and place the mold in a larger baking pan filled with 1 inch of hot water. Bake the pudding for 50 to 60 minutes, until a toothpick inserted in the center comes out clean. Remove from oven and let cool. Refrigerate for at least 4 hours.

TO SERVE: Loosen the edges with a knife and invert the pudding onto a plate. Add ½ cup water to the caramel on the bottom of the mold and place over low heat until it melts. Cool slightly and pour over the pudding.

Ambrosia

Ambrosia

8 SERVINGS

A FAVORITE DESSERT OF MANY BRAZILIAN GAÚCHOS and their families is ambrosia. It is made with sugar, cinnamon, cloves and eggs and enjoyed by people of all classes. You will find it on the menus of most restaurants.

4 CUPS SUGAR	6 EGGS
2 STICKS CINNAMON PLUS	6 EGG YOLKS
ADDITIONAL FOR GARNISH	4 CUPS MILK
3 WHOLE CLOVES	JUICE OF 1 LEMON

Place the sugar, cinnamon sticks, and cloves in a medium-size pot. Add 2 cups water and place over high heat, stirring with a wooden spoon until the sugar dissolves. Reduce the heat and cook until the mixture reaches the soft ball stage (240°F).

Meanwhile, beat the eggs and yolks together and strain through a cheesecloth. Add the milk and lemon juice (in order to make the mixture curdle). Add the egg mixture to the pot and cook over high heat, stirring until lumps form. Lower the heat and simmer, stirring occasionally, to keep the mixture from sticking, about 20 minutes, or until the mixture thickens. Pour into a deep 1-quart dish, let cool and refrigerate.

Serve cold in individual dishes with cinnamon sticks.

NOTE: The dessert should look like golden lumpy oatmeal. If you want a darker color cook it for an additional 5 minutes, stirring to keep the mixture from sticking.

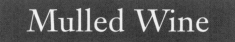
Mulled Wine

Vinho Quente
6 SERVINGS

THE COLD WINTERS OF THE SOUTH invite residents to take advantage of the region's extensive wine production by preparing this mulled wine. It's great to warm their innards on blustery days and for holiday celebrations with family and friends.

1 CUP SUGAR	1 SMALL GRANNY SMITH APPLE,
2 TEASPOONS GROUND CINNAMON	PEELED AND SLICED
5 WHOLE CLOVES	½ CUP BRANDY
4 CUPS DRY RED WINE	

Place ½ cup of the sugar, ½ cup water, the cinnamon, and cloves in a small pot over high heat and stir continually until the sugar melts and begins to turn a light golden color.

Add the wine and ½ cup water and bring to a boil. Add the remaining sugar and the apple and cook, stirring until the sugar dissolves. Remove from the heat, add the brandy, and serve in ceramic mugs.

Menus

Brazilian Party Buffet
Black-Eyed Pea Fritters – *Acarajé*
Chicken Pastries – *Empadinhas de Galinha*
Beef Croquettes – *Bolinhos de Carne*
Fried Fish Cubes with Garden Sauce – *Iscas de Pirarucu ao Molho Floresta*
Gaucho Meatballs – *Almôndegas à Moda Gaúcho*
Rice Balls – *Bolinhos de Arroz*
Chocolate Bonbons – *Brigadeiros*
Golden Coconut Cupcakes – *Quindins*
Well-Married Cookies – *Casadinhos*
Rum Cocktails – *Caipirinhas*

Northern Region Dinner
Plantain Chips – *Banana-pacova em Rodelas*
Fish Balls – *Bolinhos de Pirarucu*
Shrimp and Brazil Nut Soup – *Crème de Camarão ao Leite de Castanha*
Barbecued Fish with Bean Salad and Jambu Rice – *Filhote Pai-d' égua*
Tapioca Pudding – *Pudim de Tapioca*

Northeastern Region Dinner
Shrimp Empanadas – *Empadas de Camarão*
Spicy Greens – *Efó*
White Rice
Toasted Manioc Meal with Palm Oil – *Farofa de Azeite-de-Dendem*
Rum Cocktail – *Caipirinha*

Southeastern Region Buffet Party
Heart of Palm Pastries – *Pastéis de Palmito*
Cornmeal and Beef Pastries – *Pastéis de Farinha de Milho e Bife*
Bean Purée with Sausages – *tutu à Mineira*
Trooper Beans – *Feijão Tropeiro*
Minas Gerais-Style Greens – *Couve à Mineira*
Rice Salad – *Salada de Arroz*
Minas Cheese Rolls – *Pãezinhos de Queijo*
Manioc and Peanut Meal – *Paçoca de Amendoim*
Pumpkin and Dried Beef Torte – *Bolo de Quibebe*
Half-Moon Cookies – *Biscoitos meia-lua*

Manioc Pudding – *Pudim de Manioca*
Rum Drinks – *Batidas Paulistas*

CENTER WEST REGION DINNER
Goiás Meat and Cheese Pies – *Empadão Goiano*
Rice with Palm Hearts – *Arroz com Guariroba*
Grilled Steaks – *Bisteca na Chapa*
Manioc Biscuits – *Caburé*
Miniature Caramel Tarts – *Pastelinho*
Rum Drinks – *Batidas Paulistas*

SOUTHERN REGION BUFFET
Gaucho Meatballs – *Almôndegas à Moda Gaúcho*
Red Pepper Antipasto – *Antepasto de pimentão à Gaúcho*
Rice Balls – *Bolinhos de Arroz*
Brazilian Barbecue - *Churrasco*
Mule-Driver's Rice – *Arroz de Carreteiro*
Grilled Squabs on Skewers - *Galeto*
Ambrosia - *Ambrosia*
Mulled Wine – *Vinho Quente*

Glossary

ACARAJÉ…Black-eyed pea fritters are very popular in Brazil, especially in Salvador, Bahia. Yoruba slaves brought the recipe from Nigeria, where the fritter is called *acará*. The Brazilian name derives from the fact that women hawking the fritters on the streets of Salvador would cry *"acara je." Je* is the Yoruba word for "eat." Hence, they were yelling, "eat acará." The batter is made by peeling and grinding the peas and then mixing them with ground onions, dried shrimp and garlic. The batter is fried in palm oil.

BACALHAU…Better known as salt cod, the fish is salted at sea and brought back to the mainland to air dry. The Portuguese took this fish to Brazil, its African colonies, and to territories in the Far East. It has become part of each of these local cuisines. In Brazil it is said that there are 365 ways to prepare this fish.

BATIDA…A popular Brazilian drink enjoyed through the country. It is made with *cachaça*, a liquor made from sugarcane juice and served over crushed ice with a bit of lemon juice and lightly beaten egg whites.

CACHAÇA…A type of brandy distilled from sugarcane juice. *Cachaça* is often translated as "white rum" although the latter is actually distilled from molasses. This very Brazilian liquor is usually served plain or in cocktails known as *batidas* and *caipirinhas*.

CAMARÃO SECO (Dried shrimp)…Fresh shrimp are skewered and left to dry in the sun. When dry, they are often ground and used in Brazilian dishes for the religious festivals of *Candomblé*, an Afro-Brazilian cult. They are available in African, Asian, and Indian markets. They should be soaked in warm water before grinding.

CANDOMBLÉ…A word of African origin from the Angolan Bantu language, Kimbundu that refers to the Afro-Brazilian religion practiced in Bahia.

CARIOCA…A *Carioca* is person from the city of Rio de Janeiro. The term also refers to a cup of coffee to which a little hot water has been added.

CARNE SECA…*Carne seca* is beef that has been salted and dried in the sun. It is usually sold in 5 x 7-inch slabs about 1 inch thick. It is used in many Brazilian dishes, particularly *feijoada* and it must be soaked to desalt it before cooking. It is available in Latin American and Brazilian grocery stores.

CHOURIÇO…Dried sausages made from pork, paprika, garlic, salt, chili peppers, and red or white wine.

CHURRASCO…The Brazilian equivalent of barbecue. It is meat grilled over a charcoal fire that is also popular in northern Portugal.

CHURRASCARIAS…Barbecue restaurants that traveled from Brazil to Angola, Cape Verde, Guinea-Bissau, and Mozambique with the Portuguese. These restaurants now also exist in the U.S. and are sometimes known as *churrascarias* or *rodizios*.

COCONUT MILK…A thick, rich, milk extracted from the grated pulp of a mature coconut. It is an important ingredient in many Afro-Brazilian dishes and desserts.

COZIDO…Roughly equivalent to "stew," a dish in which meats and vegetables are covered with water and simmered. The meats and vegetables are removed and the broth is served separately as soup.

CUSCUZ (Couscous)… A dish of Arabian origin, that was brought to Portugal and Africa by the Moors. Via Africa it traveled to Brazil where it became very popular in the south, particularly São Paulo. In southern Brazil the dish is an accompaniment to the main course, and in the north couscous is a dessert.

DENDEM (also spelled Dendê)…Seeds from the African palm tree were brought to Brazil by Portuguese navigators. Dendem oil is extracted from the tree's red fruit. The oil is thick and has a reddish, yellowish color. In Brazil, the oil is used in many dishes associated with the *Candomblé* and *Macumba* religions.

EMPADA…A pastry or turnover usually stuffed with chicken, cheese, shrimp, or beef.

ESPETADA…Skewered chunks of beef, chicken or pork that are grilled over hot coals.

FAROFA…*See* Mandioca.

FEIJOADA…The national dish of Brazil. This bean stew with several varieties of meats is popular in most Portuguese-speaking countries.

MACUMBA…The name by which the Afro-Brazilian religion is known in Rio de Janeiro.

MANDIOCA…Manioc, a tuber also called yucca or cassava in the United States, is consumed in large quantities in Brazil. In Bahia and Rio it is known as *aipim*. It can be boiled, fried, or mashed, and is often used in stews. *Farinha*, the flour made from this root, can be toasted to make a *farofa* or sprinkled over beans or meats in a *feijoada* or *moqueca*. It is also used in dishes in Cape Verde, Angola, Mozambique, Guinea-Bissau, and São Tomé ans Principe.

MOQUECA…A word probably of Brazilian Indian (Tupi Guarani) origin for a type of stew made with fish or seafood seasoned with onions, green pepper, tomatoes, palm oil, and malagueta peppers.

PALMITO…The heart of the palm tree, used in stews, salads, and as an *empada* filling throughout Brazil.

PIMENTA-MALAGUETA…A small hot red pepper native to Brazil and later transported to Angola, Mozambique, and other parts of Africa.

QUIABO…Okra or lady fingers, an essential vegetable in many of the Brazilian dishes served during the religious festivals of *Candomblé*. It is also an important ingredient in dishes in other Portuguese-speaking countries such as Guinea-Bissau, Angola, and Mozambique.

REFOGADO…A sauté of vegetables, usually onions, tomatoes, and green peppers cooked until the onions are translucent. The sauce is used as a basis for various dishes.

ROUPA-VELHA…Literally "old clothes," a dish made with leftovers such as stewed or grilled beef mixed with a sauce or a *refogado*.

SEPHARDIM…Sephardim are the descendants of Jews from the Iberian Peninsula who were expelled in 1497. Many Sephardic Jews settled in Brazil and their customs and traditions, including food cultures, merged with and influenced those of their new homeland.

TOUCINHO…Fresh or salted pork belly that is used in stews or fried like bacon.

Ingredient Sources

CALIFORNIA:
Liborio Markets Brazilian Products
864 S. Vermont Avenue
Los Angeles, CA 90005
(213) 386-1458

Liborio Markets Brazilian Products
6061 Atlantic Boulevard
Maywood, CA 90270
(213) 560-8000

VIA Brazil
1770-A Lombard Street
San Francisco, CA 94123
(415) 673-7744

Mo Hotta, Mo Betta
P.O. Box 4136
San Luis Obispo, CA 93403
(800) 462-3220
Fax (805) 545-8389

ILLINOIS:
El Mercado Meat Market
3767 N. Southport Avenue
Chicago, Il 60613
(312) 477-5020

L & L Distributing Co.
1456 North Dayton
Chicago, Il 60622
(312) 915-5911
Fax (312) 915-0466

MINNESOTA:
El Burrito Mercado
Latin American Foods
175 Concord Street
St. Paul, MN 55107
(651) 227-2192

El Jalepeño Market:
Latin American Foods
7636 Lyndale Avenue South
Richfield, MN 55417
(612) 866-7600

Lagoa African Market, Inc.
1317 East Lake Street
Minneapolis, MN 55406
(612) 721-2035

Morgan's Mexican Lebanese Foods
763 S. Robert Street
St. Paul, MN 55107
(651) 291-2955

MISSOURI:
Tropicana Market
5001 Lindenwood Street
St Louis, MO 63109
(314) 353-7328

NEW JERSEY:
Seabra Super Market
119 Ferry Street
Newark, NJ 07105
(201) 589-5008

NEW YORK:
M & M Market and Deli
529 Broome Street
New York, NY 10013
(212) 219-2619

Grand Street Deli and Market
42 Grand Street
New York, NY 10013
(212) 625-3248

NEW MEXICO:
Bueno Foods
2001 4th Street S.W.
Albuquerque, NM 87102
(800) 952-4453
Fax: (505) 242-1680

RHODE ISLAND:
Gaipo's Meat Market
1075 South Broadway
East Providence, RI 02914
(401) 438-3545

Carniçaria Internacional
Lonsdale Avenue
Central Falls, RI 02863
(401) 728-9000

TENNESSEE:
The Global Market
918 Vine Street
Nashville, TN 37214
(615) 242-8593

International Grocery Store
900 8th Avenue N. (Farmer's Market)
Nashville, TN 37203
(615) 254-3697

VIRGINIA:
European Foods Import-Export, Inc.
2700 North Pershing Drive
Arlington, VA 22201
(703) 524-2856, (703) 524-6800
Fax: (703) 524-6801

Bibliography

A Culinária Baiana no Restaurante Senac Pelourinho. São Paulo, Brasil: Editora Senac Nacional, 2nd ed., 1999.

Almeida, Anabela. *Sopas Caseiras*. Lisboa, Portugal: Lusomundo, 3a edição, 2003.

Alves Filho, Ivan, and Roberto DiGiovanni. *Cozinha Brasileira com Recheio de História*. Rio de Janeiro: Editora Revan Ltda., 2000.

Andrade, Margarette de. *Brazilian Cookery, Traditional and Modern*. Rio de Janeiro: A Casa do Livro Eldorado, 1975.

Barbosa, Tereza Maria. *A Cozinha Baiana*. São Paulo: Companhia Melhoramentos, 2001.

Barbosa, Veranúbia. *Uma Receita de Saúde*. Bahia, Salvador: Edição do autor, 2001.

Brandão, Darwin. *A Cozinha Baiana*. Rio de Janeiro: Editora Letrase Artes. 1965.

Cascudo, Luis da Câmara. *A Cozinha Africana no Brasil*. Luanda: Impresa Nacional de Angola, 1964.

Costa, Dona Lena de Oliveira. *Cozinha da Roça, Delícias do Brasil Interiorano*. São Paulo: Editora Nova Alexandria Ltda., 1998.

Costa, Paloma Jorge Amado. *O Livro de Cozinha de Pedro Archanjo*. São Paulo: Editora Maltese, 1994.

Culinária Amazônica: O Sabor da Natureza. Rio de Janeiro: Editora Senac Nacional, 2000.

Culinária Nordestina, Encontro de Mar e Sertão. Rio de Janeiro: Editora Senac Nacional, 2001.

David, Suzy. *The Sephardic Kosher Kitchen*. Middle Village, New York: Jonathan David Publishers, Inc., 1984

Do Pampa à Serra: Os Sabores da Terra Gaúcha. Rio de Janeiro: Editora Senac Nacional, 1999.

Dos Comes e Bebes do Espirito Santo, A Culinária Capixaba no Hotel Ilha do Bói. Rio de Janeiro: Editora Senac Nacional, 2002.

Favero, Maria Luiza. *Receitas Práticas com Milho*. São Paulo: Companhia Melhoramentos, 1997.

Fernandes, Caloca. *A Culinária Paulista Tradicional nos Hotéis Senac São Paulo. São Paulo: 1998*.

Fernandes, Caloca. *Viagem Gastronômica através do Brasil*. São Paulo: Editora Senac Nacional, 2000.

Goldberg, Betty S. *International Cooking for the Kosher Home*. Middle Village, New York: Jonathan David Publishers, Inc., 1990.

Hamilton, Cherie Y. *Cuisines of Portuguese Encounters*. New York: Hippocrene Books, Inc., 2001.

Houaiss, Antonio. *Minhas Receitas Brasileiras*. São Paulo: Art Editora, 1990.

Japur, Jamile. *Cozinha Brasileira de Norte a Sul*. São Paulo: Editora ESSO, 1968.

Kadunc, Alexandre, *Comida de Santo*: Tríade Editorial, 1989.

Liebman, Malvina W. *Jewish Cooking from Boston to Baghdad*. Cold Spring, New York: NighinGale Resources, 1989.

Lobo, Isabel Margarida. *Receitas da Bahia*. São Paulo: Companhia Editora Nacional, 1959.

Matogrosso, Tania Maria de. *A Cozinha Mato-Grossense*. Mato Grosso, Brasil: Melhoramentos de São Paulo, 1996.

Mazzei, Celia e Celma. *A Cozinha Caipira de Celia & Celma*. Rio de Janeiro: Nova Fronteira, 1994.

Netto, Joaquim da Costa Pinto. *Carderno de Comidas Baianas*. Rio de Janeiro: Tempo Brasileiro; Salvador: Fundação Cultural de Estado da Bahia, 1986

Nunes, Maria Lúcia Clementino and Márcia Clementino Nunes. *História de Arte da Cozinha Mineira*. Belo Horizonte, Brasil: author, 2001

Querino, Manuel. *A Arte Culinaria na Bahia*. Salvador, Bahia: Livraria Progresso Editora, 1951. (Primeira edição, 1928).

Sabores e Cores das Minas Gerais: A Culinaria Mineira no Hotel Senac Grogotó. Rio de Janeiro: Editora Senac Nacional, 1999.

Santos, Aldaci Dada dos. *Tempero da Dada*. Salvador, Bahia: Editora Corrupio, 1998.

Somma, Iolanda. *Pratos Típicos, Regionais do Brasil*. Rio de Janeiro: Ediouro, 1979.

English Index

BRAZIL | A CULINARY JOURNEY

BRAZIL | A CULINARY JOURNEY

W

Portuguese Index

A

Acarajé 41
Almondegas à Moda Gaúcho 161
Aluá de Milho 33
Ambrosia 1781
Antepasto de Pimentão à Gaúcho 158
Aperitivos
    Acarajé 41
    Almondegas à Moda Gaúcho 161
    Antepasto de Pimentão à Gaúcho 158
    Banana-pacova em Rodelas 13
    Bolinhos de Arroz 160
    Bolinhos de Arroz com Sardinhas 43
    Bolinhos de Carne 46
    Bolinhos de Macaxeira Recheado 49
    Bolinhos de Pirarucu 14
    Empadão Goiano 134
    Empadas de Camarão 44
    Empadinhas de Galinha 92
    Iscas de Pirarucu ao Molho Floresta 15
    Pasteis de Farinha de Milho e Bife 94
    Pasteis de Palmito 91
    Saltenhas 132
Arroz
    Arroz Brasileira 73
    Arroz com Brócolos 76
    Arroz com Guariroba 146
    Arroz com Lingüiça 175
    Arroz com Pêssagos 176
    Arroz da Serra 120
    Arroz de Carreteiro 177
    Arroz de Haussá 74
    Arroz de Jambu 23
    Arroz de Puta Rica 147

Arroz (continued)
    Arroz Maria Isabel 77
    Bolinhos de Arroz 160
    Bolinhos de Arroz com Sardinhas 43
    Salad de Arroz 119

B

Bagre Ensopado 171
Banana-pacova em Rodelas 13
Bebidas
    Aluá de Milho 33
    Batida de Ananas 127
    Batida de Café 127
    Batida de Leite de Côco 127
    Batida Paulista 127
    Caipirinha 87
    Chocolate com Gemas 86
    Vinho Quente 182
Barreado 168
Batida Paulista 127
Bifes Enrolados 99
Biscoitos Meia-lua 124
Bisteca na Chapa 142
Bobó de Camarão 66
Bolinhos de Arroz 160
Bolinhos de Arroz com Sardinhas 43
Bolinhos de Carne 46
Bolinhos de Macaxeira Recheado 49
Bolinhos de Pirarucu 14
Bolo de Quibebe 102
Bolo de Rolo 83
Bolo Souza Leão 82
Brigadeiros 126

C

D

E

F

G

I

L

M

O

P

From Hippocrene's Latin American Cookbook Library

Aprovecho
A MEXICAN-AMERICAN BORDER COOKBOOK
Teresa Cordero Cordell and Robert Cordell
This cookbook celebrates the food and culture found along the Mexican Border. It offers more than 250 recipes from appetizers and beverages to entrees and desserts, combining a tantalizing array of ingredients from both sides of the border. Easy-to-follow instructions enable cooks to create a special dish or an entire fiesta in no time. The book contains informative sections ranging from how tequila is made, making tamales, and a guide to Mexican beer.
400 PAGES • 6 X 10 • 0-7818-1026-4 • $24.95HC • (554)

Argentina Cooks!
TREASURED RECIPES FROM THE NINE REGIONS OF ARGENTINA (EXPANDED EDITION)
Shirley Lomax Brooks
Argentine cuisine is one of the world's best-kept culinary secrets. The country's expansive landscape includes tropical jungles, vast grasslands with sheep and cattle, alpine lakes and glacier-studded mountains. As a result, a great variety of foods are available—game, lamb, an incredible assortment of fish and seafood, exotic fruits and prime quality beef. This cookbook highlights the food from Argentina's nine regions in 190 recipes, including signature dishes from Five Star chefs, along with the best recipes from the author and other talented home chefs. Along with insight into Argentina's landscape, history, traditions and culture, this cookbook includes a section on Argentine wines.
314 PAGES • 6 X 9 • 0-7818-0997-5 • $24.95HC • (384)

Mexican Culinary Treasures Recipes from Maria Elena's Kitchen
Maria Elena C. Lorens
WITH A FOREWORD BY MARILYN TAUSEND, AUTHOR OF *SAVORING MEXICO* AND *COCINA DE LA FAMILIA*
Mexican Culinary Treasures contains 166 recipes, from the very traditional to the nouvelle cuisine of cosmopolitan Mexico City. This fascinating volume offers cooks and readers an in-depth look into Mexican cooking and the history behind it. Maria Elena C. Lorens combines an extensive knowledge of Mexico's traditions with a personal flair and enthusiasm that encourages people to cross cultural boundaries and taste evocative new flavors.
250 PAGES • 6 X 9 • 0-7818-1061-2 • $24.95HC • (107) • OCTOBER

My Mother's Bolivian Kitchen

RECIPES AND RECOLLECTIONS

José Sánchez-H.

My Mother's Bolivian Kitchen includes 150 unique recipes, as well as a memoir of growing up in a culture where eating is taken quite seriously. The recipes presented in this book are easy to make and, although some of the ingredients are not available in the United States, the author provides substitutions to achieve similar results.

Bolivian cuisine is quite distinct from that of many Latin American countries, both in preparation and ingredients. It incorporates foods developed by the Incas, such as quinoa and *chuño* (freeze-dried potato). Among the recipes included is a Bolivian pastry, called *salteñas*; its warm golden crust, when broken open, releases a pungent smell of exotically spiced meat, vegetables, and raisins.

300 PAGES • 6 X 9 • 0-7818-1056-6 • $24.95HC • (65) • NOVEMBER

Secrets of Colombian Cooking

Patricia McCausland-Gallo

From the coffee and cacao grown high in the Andes Mountains to the many tropical fruits of the Caribbean and Amazonian regions, the great cattle farms on the plains, and bountiful seafood from the Pacific Ocean and the Caribbean Sea, Colombia is a country of vast and exotic culinary creations. Secrets of Colombian Cooking presents the wide spectrum of Colombian cuisine to home cooks in more than 175 inviting recipes from simple, hearty *sancochos* (soups and stews prepared differently in every region) to more exotic fare such as *Langosta al Coco* (lobster in coconut sauce) and *Ají de Uchuvas* (Yellow Gooseberry Sauce).

270 PAGES • 6 X 9 • 0-7818-1025-6 • $24.95HC • (560)

A Taste of Haiti (Expanded Edition)

Mirta Yurnet-Thomas & The Thomas Family

African, French, Arabic and Amerindian influences make the food and culture of Haiti fascinating subjects to explore. From the days of slavery to present times, traditional Haitian cuisine has relied upon staples such as root vegetables, pork, fish, and flavor enhancers like *Pikliz* (picklese, or hot pepper vinegar) and *Zepis* (ground spices). This cookbook presents more than 100 traditional Haitian recipes, which are complemented by information on Haiti's history, holidays and celebrations, staple foods, and cooking methods. Recipe titles are presented in English, Creole, and French.

180 PAGES • 5½ X 8½ • 0-7818-0998-3 • $24.95HC • (588)